MW00509700

# FOUNDATIONS FOR SUCCESS

## EIGHT WEEKS TO REAL ESTATE SUCCESS

# VOLUME 6
# WORKBOOK

**Stephen L. Silver, BScPT**

Broker

Copyright © 2015 Stephen L. Silver
All rights reserved.

This book, or parts thereof, may not be reproduced in any form without the express written permission of the author.

This publication is designed to provide information with regard to the subject matter covered.  It is sold with the understanding that the author and publisher are not engaged in rendering legal, accounting or other professional advice. If legal advice or other expert assistance is required, the services of a competent professional person should be sought.

ISBN 13:  978-0-9939401-7-0

# BUSINESS BUILDING EXERCISES

"One of life's most painful moments comes when we must admit that we didn't do our homework, that we are not prepared."

Merlin Olsen

# Contents

# Foreword

Recently a new Salesperson revealed to me what most newly licensed individuals experience... *"Bruce, when I got my real estate license, it seemed like they gave me the keys to the car but then nobody taught me how to drive it."* There's a lot of wisdom in that analogy and...no doubt a lot of frustration for people starting out.

In his first book, **List to Last**, Stephen Silver focused on prospecting for, closing on and managing listings. In his second book, **Foundations for Success**, Steve takes you through a very detailed process of "how to drive a car." As a new REALTOR®, you need to take time to develop your business without wasting time and money. You'll learn how to:

- Develop a simple business plan that will take you on the trip from where you are now to where you want to be.
- Avoid the most common traps in which new REALTORS® get caught.
- Implement the systems that help you:
  - Become organized, in terms of managing time, finances and clients.
  - Connect with and cultivate the leads you'll need to develop in order to secure a consistent, reproducible business.
  - Manage listings and buyers from start to finish.

This book provides specific business building exercises for you to complete that will utilize the information provided and get you on track to success fast. You'll see how you can achieve the success you deserve and grow your business at a significantly greater rate than you ever thought.

I have known Steve Silver for a long time... he knows the business inside out and is an excellent "driving instructor." Follow these steps, take them on chapter by chapter and you too will be "a great driver". Good luck...turn the key and start your engine!

Bruce Keith

---

Bruce Keith is a leading Motivational Speaker and Trainer for sales organizations in North America, specializing in Real Estate Sales.

He has been in real estate in excess of 27 years, including 16 years as a top Coach for thousands of Sales Agents. Learn more at www.BruceKeithResults.com.

# Acknowledgements

Bruce Keith, mentor, coach and long-time friend, for sharing his experience, his encouragement and recommendations, which made the publishing of this series possible.

Aileen Simcic, my best friend and business partner, for her support and encouragement through the many years of our shared real estate practice and beyond and her husband, Christopher Hairrell, for putting up with it all.

Bohdan Uszkalo, friend, business partner and general wild and crazy guy, who always had a joke (not always great) and an encouraging word.

Gerald Tostowaryk, whose personal and professional life defines the meaning of ethics and character and who kept me pointed in the right direction when I needed it.

Dan Gitzel, friend, Broker and mentor, who gave me the chance to find my way back to what I love, teaching and helping others and without whom none of this would have been possible.

David Yunker, ever present and ever available friend, mentor and sounding board, without whose guidance and advice this work would have oft gone astray.

Virginia Munden whose example of dedication to teaching and mentoring has been an inspiration and for taking the time from her ridiculously busy schedule to help me get this book into a readable condition.

# ACKNOWLEDGEMENTS

George Zanette, friend and trusted advisor, whose advice has been instrumental in getting this book into a format that makes sense to more people than just me.

Christina Davie, friend, major support and chief architect of my endurance, without whom I would have either called it quits or be sitting in prison for murder.

Josie Stern, friend, inspiration and SuperREALTOR®, for demonstrating, on a daily basis, that the main thesis of this book, having and consistently using systems as well as an unwavering commitment to client service, are the only ways to succeed in real estate.

And finally, but most importantly, to my family, my father Gerald, and daughters Arielle and Andrea, who endured my neglect, ordered in food, and my mood swings and still gave me their unrelenting support, encouragement and love. Without you, this would never have been possible.

# Introduction

## Systems for Success

Real estate sales can be a siren song to many. To those outside the business it appears to be an easy way to make money. Watch any of the home improvement channels and you can see people flipping this house, flipping that house, real estate agents selling million dollar properties to the first people that walk in the door, turning junk homes into gorgeous properties and renting them out to the first group through. And all this happens during an hour long show. So many get into the business with the dream of earning a huge income in their first few months, but it's a sad fact of life in the real estate world that almost 50% of new Sales Representatives fail and are out of the business within the first year of graduating from the training programs. And a further 50% of the remaining aspirants drop out within the second year.

This happens for a wide range of reasons, but the most common one is that the initial training programs don't adequately educate them on the realities of life in the real world as a REALTOR®. They're taught how to avoid getting into trouble with the provincial regulators. They're taught the basics of real estate law and they're taught such useful tools as the length of a "chain", metes and bounds or the Torrens system. There's little to no training on what is truly necessary to succeed in this most competitive business, systems.

That's why this series has been written. It's designed to provide new salespeople with the information, tools, skills and systems they'll require to help them get through those first couple of difficult years.

In this series can be found a step by step approach to implementing the systems that every successful real estate salesperson requires, beginning with business planning and time management and moving through organizational systems, prospecting, working with sellers and buyers and much more. Tools and business building exercises are included, both in the series, the workbook and online at www.foundationsforsuccess.ca which will assist the salesperson in developing those systems, their skills and confidence.

**Volume 1 – On the Right Foot** will introduce you to the Business Plan, the real secret behind getting started without falling into the traps encountered by most new Sales Representatives. It will also introduce you to the key components of success, consistency and organization; doing what needs to be done, when it needs to be done, as often as it needs to be done, in every aspect of the business, including time, client and financial management.

**Volume 2 – Good Hunting** will familiarize you with various types of prospecting techniques, and even more importantly than the types of techniques, you'll learn to develop the mindset required to be consistently successful at it. You'll be shown how to develop and maintain one of the most important long-term prospecting activities, a farm, an activity which will establish you as the best known and most knowledgeable REALTOR® in the area. We'll review the many different active forms that prospecting may take, including making prospecting calls, door-knocking, Open Houses, converting For Sale By Owners, networking, trade shows, and participating in client and community events.

Volume 2 will examine not just lead generation but will also help you develop a complete and organized lead follow up system, so that the leads you generate result in ongoing and future business. You'll read about how to follow up with leads rapidly, effectively and to set them up on a program that keeps you in touch with them until they're ready to act.

In **Volume 3 – Listings, Listings, Listings** you'll read about, and prepare a listing system that differentiates you from other REALTORS® and helps influence people to want to work with you before they actually meet you. It discusses listing presentations that demonstrate to the potential client that you're able to provide them with the value they're seeking and what they feel is important, not what you believe your value is. You'll also learn to develop a highly organized listing system that ensures you follow a consistent process for every listing, thereby reducing or eliminating the possibility of missing any steps throughout the entire sales cycle.

Volume 3 will also review and discuss offer management, a key component of a well-constructed listing system. The management of offers, both single and multiple, can easily become disorganized and chaotic without a standardized method of handling the many aspects of what can be a complex procedure.

In **Volume 4 – Buyers, Buyers, Buyers** you'll read about different buyer demographics, what the average buyer in each is looking for when purchasing a home and the questions that will help you determine what your client is looking for, what type of buyer they are and that will help you narrow down their needs and wants. By following the systems in this volume, you should be able to review the properties for which they're looking and help you find them the right property in the least amount of time.

As in Volume 3, this volume will help you develop a buyers' system, including an offer management system for your buyer which will enable you to protect your client's interests while obtaining the property with the least amount of difficulty.

And in **Volume 5 – I'm Just Sayin'**, you'll be introduced to a critical skill you'll need to develop, objection handling. Using the BASIQ technique, introduced in this volume, you'll be able to quickly and easily determine what the true objection is and by asking the right questions and listening carefully to the answers you'll have the opportunity to understand what the client's concern is and, even more, how to handle it.

The next critical skill you'll need to cultivate is your communication abilities, in order to eliminate the major source of complaints against REALTORS®, a lack of communication or a miscommunication that was never resolved. This volume will discuss how your ongoing task will be to, through the use of open ended questions and active listening techniques, fully grasp what your client is trying to communicate to you as well as ensuring that the client is able to clearly hear and understand the information you're providing.

You'll also be introduced to negotiation, which, if not prepared for, can be a very disconcerting experience. You'll learn how to work towards a win-win resolution, how to prepare for the negotiation and how to develop and execute an effective game plan, complete with specific strategies to achieve the desired outcomes.

And last, this volume will provide you with direction on marketing and advertising. As with any other system, your marketing strategy must planned out for the year so that you don't miss any component or spend money where you needn't, a major point of failure for most new salespeople. You'll learn how to write ads that appeal to buyers.

And finally **Volume 6 – The Workbook** will provide you with a weekly, step by step approach to building and managing your business. You'll have opportunities to develop, in a logical, proven, sequence by completing the exercises provided, the systems, skills, and tools you'll need to smooth out the learning curve, reduce the time required to implement the systems needed to ensure their success and begin earning a steady, reproducible and predictable income in a shorter period of time.

However, it is not the end of what you need to do and what you need to learn. As with any athlete, learning the rudiments of the sport is just the beginning. Stop learning and perfecting your skills and techniques and you end up being nothing more than average at best. Professional and high caliber amateur athletes all recognize that the key to ongoing success is to have someone who can teach them and hold them accountable for their performance, forcing them to take absolute advantage of their strengths as well as to face their weaknesses and overcome them; in other words, a coach. I strongly urge you to consider working with a real estate coach who can help you hone your skills and techniques as well as provide you with additional tools and skills designed to test your limits, push you to excel and ensure you reach the goals you'll set for yourself.

# INTRODUCTION

# BUSINESS BUILDING EXERCISES

The steps you'll find in this workbook are designed to help you move forward in developing your systems, skills and confidence. They are divided according to specific time frames and highlighted to help you achieve those goals as efficiently as possible.

While still allowing you time to put the information into practise, they have been carefully structured to ensure you are able to develop the basic systems you'll need to have to ensure predictable, reproducible and consistent results. The foundations for success are all included here and, if you follow them, will provide you with an easy to follow road map to get you through what is generally the most difficult time for new salespeople.

On top of everything included here, try to attend as much training as you can fit into your schedule. Don't just attend sales related sessions. It's important to be a sponge and absorb as much information as you can about as many other topics as you can. You never know when something may come in handy.

One of the best ways to find out how to be successful is to hang around other successful agents. Just hang around and listen. Buy them a coffee and ask them how they got there. And listen. I remember when I was just starting in the business. I was almost broke and was getting to the point that I was seriously questioning whether this was really what I wanted to do or not. One of the more successful agents in our office and I happened to go out for a coffee. I'll never forget the story he told me of when he was at the same point in his career and how just doing what needed to be done consistently paid off for him. It made a huge impact and was something I tried to focus on from that point on.

Take the opportunity to sit in on conferences and seminars, like Richard Robbins' Secrets of the Masters, Brian Buffini's Success Tour and Mike Ferry's Action Workshops. Think about getting a coach, like Bruce Keith. The knowledge and skill development and accountability that having a great coach brings to the table will be career changing.

However, don't let the training distract you from completing the assignments you'll find here on time. This is the foundations for your long term success that you're building.

# WEEK 1

## 1. Create your Life Purpose Statement

Remember, this is going to be the ultimate goal for your life; what you want your legacy to be and how you want to be remembered.

Expect that this particular exercise may take you more than the first two weeks, so don't wait until you've completed this to move on to the next exercise.

### *My Life Purpose Statement*

_____

_____

_____

_____

_____

_____

_____

_____

_____

_____

_____

## 2. Develop your Mission Statement

This will be what you want the outside world, including your sphere of influence and potential clients to think of when they think of your services. I generally suggest that you think of four to six key words that describe what you believe to be your greatest customer service strengths. Then create a paragraph that uses these words as key components, for example:

"To consistently provide professional, ethical and dependable real estate services to my clients and to ensure the integration of my core values of service, flexibility, dedication, enthusiasm, and integrity into that service."

***My Key Words***

_____

_____

_____

_____

_____

_____

_____

_____

_____

_____

## <u>My Mission Statement</u>

## 3. Complete your Personal SWOT Analysis

Complete your SWOT Analysis by filling in the sections below.

### *Strengths*

_____

_____

_____

_____

_____

_____

_____

_____

_____

_____

_____

_____

_____

_____

_____

_____

_____

_____

## *Weaknesses*

_____

_____

_____

_____

_____

_____

_____

_____

_____

_____

_____

_____

_____

_____

_____

_____

_____

_____

## *Opportunities*

_____

_____

_____

_____

_____

_____

_____

_____

_____

_____

_____

_____

_____

_____

_____

_____

_____

_____

_____

_____

_____

_____

## *Threats*

_____

_____

_____

_____

_____

_____

_____

_____

_____

_____

_____

_____

_____

_____

_____

_____

_____

_____

_____

_____

_____

# WEEK 1

# WEEK 2

## 1. Business Planning

### Step 1 - Set your Goal

**Download the Business Planning Worksheets from www.foundationsforsuccess.com or use the following pages in the workbook. Enter your Income goal for the year.** Most new Sales Representatives only achieve 60 – 75% of their target. Set the bar high but make sure it's attainable.

**Enter the Average Commission for transactions in your area.** If you're a new Sales Representative and don't have any previous commissions to base your goals on, ask your broker/manager for assistance with the average commissions for the brokerage.

**Divide the Income by the Commission to determine the number of transactions required.**

| INCOME GOAL | AVERAGE COMMISSION | TRANSACTIONS NEEDED |
|---|---|---|
| $ _____ | $ _____ | _____ |

## Step 2 - Listings or Buyers

Enter the percentage of your business you want to come from Listings and from Buyers.

| LISTINGS | BUYERS |
|---|---|
| % | % |

Using the percentages you entered above and the number of transactions needed, **calculate the number of total listings and buyers needed to reach your goal.**

| TRANSACTIONS NEEDED | PERCENTAGE FROM LISTINGS | PERCENTAGE FROM BUYERS |
|---|---|---|
| | % | % |
| | TOTAL SOLD LISTINGS NEEDED | TOTAL SOLD BUYERS NEEDED |
| | | |

## Step 3 – How Many Appointments Needed

### *Listings*

**Enter the number of sold listings needed from above.**

**Total Sold Listings needed**        _____

**Enter your Listings taken to Listings Sold ratio.**

It's been my experience that for new Sales Representatives, the following averages are generally appropriate:

Listings Taken to Listings Sold Ratio      50 – 60%

**Your Listings Taken to Listings Sold Ratio**    _____ %

**Total Listings Required**      _____

It's been my experience that for new Sales Representatives, the following averages are generally appropriate:

# of Listing Appointments needed for each
Listing Taken        5 - 7

**# of Listing Appointments needed for each
Listing Taken**       _____

**Number of Listing Appointments needed
(Total Listings needed x # of
appointments/listing)**      _____

## *Purchases*

**Enter the number of Sold Buyers required from the chart above.**

**Total Buyers Needed** _____

It's been my experience that for new Sales Representatives, the following averages are generally appropriate:

Written to Close Percentage                    75 - 80%

**Your Written to Close Percentage**    _____ %

**Number of Written Contracts needed (Total Buyers needed x Written to Close ratio)**                    _____

**Enter the number of contacts required for each appointment.**

Averages

Contacts needed for each Appointment ($1^{st}$ year)                    120 – 130

$2^{nd}$ - $5^{th}$ year                    50 - 60

$6^{th}$ year +                    30 - 40

**Contacts Required per Appointment**    _____

**Total Appointments Needed (Listing + Buyer Appointments)**                    _____

**Total Yearly Contacts Required**    _____

**Total Daily Contacts Required,** Working 225 Days per Year                    _____

## Step 4 - Create Your Task List

Now that you've calculated the number of contacts you're going to need to make, you'll need to create your task list to define from what sources you'll develop business.

### *Your 3 Point Stool*

As discussed in *Volume 1 – On the Right Foot*, this is where you'll choose your 3 point stool; the three sources which you believe will produce the best opportunities for developing your business. The first of these should always be through the use of referrals from past clients, your Sphere of Influence and repeat clients.

**Using the Business Planning Worksheets or the following page, complete the chart, indicating how many transactions you intend to complete for each of the sources you've chosen to pursue and how many you plan on for each quarter.**

# WEEK 2

**Goal: Generate _____ Transactions**

| Source of Business | Number of Transactions | Quarterly Target | |
|---|---|---|---|
| Referrals from Past Clients / Sphere of Influence & Repeat Clients | | Q1 Q3 | Q2 Q4 |
| Open Houses | | Q1 Q3 | Q2 Q4 |
| Website / Social Media | | Q1 Q3 | Q2 Q4 |
| Prospecting | | Q1 Q3 | Q2 Q4 |
| Ad / Sign Calls | | Q1 Q3 | Q2 Q4 |
| Other Networking | | Q1 Q3 | Q2 Q4 |
| FSBO / Expireds | | Q1 Q3 | Q2 Q4 |
| Just Listed / Just Sold Marketing | | Q1 Q3 | Q2 Q4 |
| Commercial | | Q1 Q3 | Q2 Q4 |
| Other (Specify) | | Q1 Q3 | Q2 Q4 |

**Quarterly Targets Total**

**Q1 -          Q2 -          Q3 -          Q4 -**

# FOUNDATIONS FOR SUCCESS

## Define your Tactical Plan

a. Using the Business Planning Worksheet, list the objectives for each source of business you plan on utilizing.

b. **Enter the number of transactions and the source of business you'll be using in the "Task" field**, i.e. Task – 3 Transactions – Referrals.

c. Using the SWOT Analysis you completed earlier, **list each of the assignments you'll need to complete and when your deadline for completion will be.** Remember, each objective takes into account your strengths and opportunities and how you'll use them to achieve each task as well as your weaknesses and the education, skills, tools and people you'll need to help you overcome them.

| Task – 3 Referrals from SOI | | Deadline | Achieved |
|---|---|---|---|
| Objective - Complete Database | | Jan. 31 | |
| 1 | Create Database of friends, family and past clients | Jan. 10 | |
| 2 | Implement Contact Management System | Jan. 15 | |
| 3 | Upload Database to CRM System | Jan. 18 | |
| 4 | Contact SOI and Qualify / Eliminate | Jan. 25 | |
| 5 | Set up Monthly Newsletter and Initiate Referral Management System | Jan. 31 | |

## 2. Complete Your Referral Database

a. **Download the Excel spreadsheet named "Database" from www.foundationsforsuccess.com.**

b. **Enter as many people you know and who know you by first name as possible.** Do NOT edit anyone out; include everyone. Use the following chart to include people about whom you may not have thought, but who should be included.

c. **Save the file as a CSV file** for export to your Client Retention Management System at a later date.

### *Who do you know?*

**Who do you know that is a(n)...**

| | | |
|---|---|---|
| Aerobics Instructor | Airline Employee | Attorney |
| Barber | Beautician | Business Owner |
| Cashier | Caterer | Chiropractor |
| Dentist | Dietitian | Doctor |
| | | Executive |
| Educator | Engineer | Assistant |
| Financial Planner | Florist | Fundraiser |
| Insurance salesperson | Interior decorator | Limo driver |
| Massage therapist | Nurse | Office worker |
| Orthodontist | Physical therapist | PR agent |
| Project manager | Retired executive | Sales Rep |
| Telemarketer | Veteran | Waitress |

# FOUNDATIONS FOR SUCCESS

**Who sold you or services your...**

| | | |
|---|---|---|
| Alarm system | Bicycle | Bed |
| Boat | Books | Bridal gown |
| Camera | Camper | Car |
| Carpeting | Clothing | Computer |
| Condominium | Construction | Copier |
| Cosmetics | Dry cleaning | Exercise equipment |
| Fence | Formal wear | Fruit |
| Furniture | Gas | Horse |
| Manicure | Mobile phone | Mortgage |
| Motorcycle | Music | Mutual funds |
| Office supplies | Payroll | Pet supplies |
| Photography | Piano | Pool |
| Printing | Quilting materials | Refrigerator |
| Rental Equipment | Roofing | Secretarial |
| Stereo system | Shoe repair | Sporting goods |
| Tax return | Tires | Tools |
| Travel | | |

**Other people...**

| | |
|---|---|
| Parents/grandparents | Brother/sister/in law |
| Aunts/Uncles/Cousins | Past jobs |
| Coworkers | High school friends |

**People you grew up with**

| | | |
|---|---|---|
| College friends | Neighbors | Play sports with |

**Who do you know at ...**

| | | |
|---|---|---|
| Bingo | Book club | Bowling |
| Camp | Child care | Chamber of commerce |

# WEEK 2

| | | |
|---|---|---|
| Clubs | Government | Place of worship |
| Golf course | Garden center | Health club |
| Hospital | Hotel | Nightclub |
| Pharmacy | Restaurant | School |
| Supermarket | Tennis | Volunteer group |
| Parents of kids friends | Kid's teachers | Military friends |
| Fraternity/sorority | Bridesmaids | Bridge players |
| Mailman\UPS\FedEx driver | | Other networkers |
| Vacation friends | | |

# WEEK 3

## 1. Learn and Practice Your Scripts (See Appendix)

a. **Use the Just Listed or Just Sold scripts** in the Appendix (or any other one you prefer to work with) and personalize it.

b. **Role play for half an hour daily** with someone at your office.

c. Use different role play partners on a rotating basis, if possible. This ensures that you get different critiques and don't get the same answers. Remember, the role play sessions should be as realistic as possible, but should also be kept positive and the critiques constructive.

## 2. Put the Scripts to Use

a. **Make 100 prospecting calls daily from Monday to Friday.**

This is, of course, to help you develop your skills and confidence but even more importantly to help you get into a consistent prospecting habit as well as find leads and prospects.

b. **Track the number of contacts you make each day** using the Contact Tracking Form you can find in the Appendix and on www.foundationsforsuccess.com.

## 3. Set Up Your Schedule

Set up a schedule that ensures you take care of the most important business when you need to take care of it, as often as you need to take care of it. Time blocking and following your schedule is a major component of successful time management.

### Step 1 – Get a Calendar

You're going to need two calendars; one wall calendar and a copy of the weekly schedule you'll find in the Appendix and on www.foundationsforsuccess.com.

**Go to your nearest office supply store and get a wall calendar for the year.** A dry erase board may be the best option. **Download the Weekly Schedule.**

Put the calendar up on your wall at the office. An electronic calendar on your mobile and computer are very handy, but there's nothing like seeing your entire schedule every day to keep you on track.

### Step 2 – Yearly Holidays

**Decide when you'll be taking your holidays and mark the time on your wall calendar** and then enter them on your mobile device and sync to your computer (or vice versa). If you don't get away at that time, you can rejig your schedule to correct the dates at a later time.

### Step 3 – R&R Time

**Set aside, at minimum, one day per week to rest and recuperate** and spend time with your family, friends or significant other. **Rule out the day on your yearly calendar and your Weekly Schedule.**

As well, set aside some time to exercise, meditate, or whatever you need to do on a daily basis to look after your own health needs.

### Step 4 – Heigh Ho, Heigh Ho, It's off to Work I Go

**Decide what time you're going to start work and when your last appointment will finish and mark this off on your weekly schedule, mobile device and computer.**

### Step 5 – Munchy Time

**Schedule time for lunch and dinner.** You need to eat and you don't want to end up eating a rushed lunch at some fast food restaurant on a regular basis, or having dinner late at night and then falling into bed. Not healthy prospects! Look after yourself first.

### Step 6 – Lead Generation

Schedule your Lead Generation / Prospecting time on your weekly schedule, mobile device and computer. Traditionally, lead generation is done in the mornings, when your energy levels are at their greatest. I would recommend that you **schedule this for at least 3 hours each morning during the week, i.e. 9:00 am – 12:00 pm.**

**Mark your quarterly Listing Appointment and Purchase Contract targets on your wall calendar at the end of each quarter.**

### Step 7 – Follow-Up Time

Lead follow up is generally managed in the early afternoon, at which time your energy is still high.

**Schedule 90 minute slots after lunch for your lead follow up.**

### Step 8 – Preview New Listings

One of the most important things you can do when starting out is to make sure you're as knowledgeable as possible on the available inventory and the best way to accomplish that is to preview them.

**Schedule at least one 90 minute appointment slot every week to preview the new listings in your office and its surrounding area.**

### Step 9 – Open Houses

One of the most effective methods of prospecting is to run effective Open Houses.

**Schedule at least one five hour time slot to run an Open Houses per weekend.**

### Step 10 – R&D Time

**Schedule two 60 - 90 minute slots for researching the market weekly.**

Take a top producer out for lunch and ask them how they got where they did. And then listen. It's amazing what you'll learn.

## Step 11 – Training & Courses

**Schedule at least one 90 minute slot every week for training, courses and/or webinars.**

## Step 12 – All the Rest

**Schedule 90 minute appointment slots** within the remaining time, giving yourself at least half an hour to get from one appointment to the next.

## The Final Step

**Post a copy of your schedule in your office, in different places at home and set it up on your mobile device and computer with reminders for each of the time blocks.**

Follow the schedule consistently.  If you don't have appointments booked, use the time constructively to work on building your business, such as prospecting, training or role playing. Do NOT use it to sit around and socialize with the other salespeople in your office. Remember, if they're sitting around and socializing, they're probably not busy and they're not the people from whom you'll learn good habits.

## *Sample Weekly Schedule (See Appendix for Blank Schedule)*

| | MONDAY | TUESDAY | WEDNESDAY | THURSDAY | FRIDAY | SATURDAY | SUNDAY |
|---|---|---|---|---|---|---|---|
| 8:00 - 8:30 am | Role Play | Role Play | Role Play | Role Play | Role Play | Role Play | OFF (Sorry I'm completely Booked) |
| 8:30 - 9:00 am | Prospecting Calls & SOI | Prospecting Calls & SOI | Prospecting Calls & SOI | Prospecting Calls & SOI | Prospecting Calls & SOI | Prospecting Calls & SOI | |
| 9:00 - 9:30 am | | | | | | | |
| 9:30 - 10:00 am | | | | | | | |
| 10:00 - 10:30 am | | | | | | | |
| 10:30 - 11:00 am | | | | | | | |
| 11:00 - 11:30 am | Appointment Available | Appointment Available | Appointment Available | Appointment Available | Appointment Available | | |
| 11:30 - 12:00 pm | | | | | | | |
| 12:00 - 12:30 pm | | | | | | Open House | |
| 12:30 - 1:00 pm | Lead Follow Up | Lead Follow Up | Lead Follow Up | Lead Follow Up | Lead Follow Up | | |
| 1:00 - 1:30 pm | | | | | | | |
| 1:30 - 2:00 pm | | | | | | | |
| 2:00 - 2:30 pm | | | | | | | |
| 2:30 - 3:00 pm | Appointment Available | Appointment Available | Appointment Available | Appointment Available | Preview New Listings | | |
| 3:00 - 3:30 pm | | | | | | | |
| 3:30 - 4:00 pm | | | | | | | |
| 4:00 - 4:30 pm | | | | Appointment Available | | | |
| 4:30 - 5:00 pm | Doorknocking (Farm) | | Doorknocking (Farm) | | Doorknocking (Farm) | | |
| 5:00 - 5:30 pm | | Appointment Available | | Appointment Available | | | |
| 5:30 - 6:00 pm | | | | | | | |
| 6:00 - 6:30 pm | | | | | | | |
| 6:30 - 7:00 pm | | | | | | | |
| 7:00 - 7:30 pm | Appointment Available | Appointment Available | Appointment Available | Appointment Available | Appointment Available | | |
| 7:30 - 8:00 pm | | | | | | | |
| 8:00 - 8:30 pm | | | | | | | |
| 8:30 - 9:00 pm | | | | | | | |

## 4. Eliminate the Time Vampires

a.  List as many of your Time Vampires (your time wasting activities and distractions) as you can.

b.  Describe how you can avoid or eliminate them (Your Garlic Bouquets).

### a.  <u>My Time Vampires</u>

_____

_____

_____

_____

_____

_____

_____

_____

_____

_____

_____

_____

_____

_____

## b. My Garlic Bouquets

_____

_____

_____

_____

_____

_____

_____

_____

_____

_____

_____

## 5. Referral Management System Part 1

**Decide on a Client Retention Management System.** Choose one that will allow you to easily and automatically maintain contact with your Sphere of Influence as well as provide a drip marketing campaign to your prospects. Do **NOT** wait until you've completed your database.

# WEEK 4

## 1. Continue Role Playing & Prospecting Calls

a.  **Continue your daily role playing sessions.**

b.  **Continue making 100 prospecting calls daily and tracking the number of contacts you make each day.** Are you making the number of contacts you need to daily? If not, you'll need to increase the number of calls you make each day.

c.  **Using the Daily Activity Tracking Form** in the Appendix or on www.foundationsforsuccess.com, track your appointments, leads and prospects.

## 2. Referral Management System Part 2

a.  **Transfer the CSV file** you created last week to your CRM system. If you haven't completed your database, transfer the people you have already entered.

b.  **Review and modify the Referral Database Qualifying Script.**

c.  **Begin calling and Qualify or Eliminate people from your Database using your script.**

d.  **Format your Monthly Newsletter**.

e.  **Implement it** for distribution to your database beginning next month.

f. **Set up your CRM system to send you birthday and home purchase anniversary reminders** for your database and past clients at least 5 days before the event.

g. **Set up several drip marketing campaigns.** These should include campaigns for the following:

    i.   30 – 60 day Seller prospects

    ii.   60 – 90 day Seller prospects

    iii.   > 90 day Seller prospects

    iv.   FSBO prospects

    v.   30 – 60 day Buyer prospects

    vi.   60 – 90 day Buyer prospects

    vii.   > 90 day Buyer prospects

    viii.   Renter to Buyer prospects

h. **Download the Referral Management System Schedule** from www.foundationsforsucces.com

i. **Complete your yearly Referral Management System Schedule** (See next page) to include:

    i.   Quarterly calls to your database - schedule these on your calendar

        •   Calculate the number of people on your database divided by the number of prospecting days in the quarter, i.e. 120 people / 60 days = 2 people per day

    ii.   Birthday cards for the homeowners

- Go to your nearest dollar store and purchase a series of generic birthday cards or sign up for a service that sends out cards for you

- Sign as many as possible to have on hand for mailing

iii. Holiday cards

- Purchase a series of major holiday cards that are appropriate to your database as well as Mother's Day, Father's Day  and Canada Day or Independence Day cards

- Sign as many as possible to have on hand for mailing

iv. Pop-bys

- Go to www.popbyideas.com for ideas

- On a seasonal basis drop off pop-bys for your database

## 3. Practice makes Perfect

a. **Find a number of available listings of all different kinds** (single family, condo, multifamily, properties with tenants, rural properties, etc.).

b. **Write offers for each of them.**

c. **Use different conditions and terms** to make them as real as possible.

d. **Have your broker/ manager check them to make sure they're accurate and realistic.**

## 4. Lead Follow Up System

a. **Download the Lead Tracking Form** from www.foundationsforsuccess.com

b. **Copy your Lead Tracking Forms** onto bright coloured paper for hot leads and white for other leads.

c. **Place them in a lead follow up binder.**

d. **Create your 8 week prospect follow-up system** based on the drip marketing campaign you established in your CRM system.

e. **Prepare your phone, text and email templates.** Remember, they need to sound like you.

f. **Create your list of qualifying questions** to use to determine a lead's motivation when you receive an ad or sign call and

g. **Role play them with a colleague** until you're comfortable with them.

# WEEK 5

## 1. Continue Role Playing & Prospecting Calls

a. **Continue your daily role playing sessions. Include Objection Handling as part of the role play.**

b. **Continue making at least 100 prospecting calls daily.**

c. **Continue tracking the number of contacts and appointments you make each day.**

## 2. Become a Farmer

a. **Decide on your farm area** based on the criteria discussed in Volume 2.

b. **Find out about the schools in the area.** How do they rank on the Fraser Institute Report Cards (Canada)? Speak to the vice-principals about the resources they have.

c. **Start walking the area and meeting the business owners.** Become the neighbourhood expert. What services are in the area? What amenities are there? What's the Walkscore for the community?

d. **Create a monthly Area Update** (See Appendix and www.foundationsforsuccess.com for a sample template) and use it for doorknocking.

e. **Develop your doorknocking dialogue** (See Appendix and www.foundationsforsuccess.com).

f. **Begin doorknocking in your farm at least 2-3 times per week using your dialogue.**

g. **Talk to 5 businesses in the area** and find out if there's a way to co-market. Begin building your Strategic Alliances.

## 3. File Management

a. **Set up 5 Listing files** with all the paperwork required by your brokerage, the New Listing Task List, Seller Questionnaire, Feedback Form, Marketing Checklist and Deal Tracking Form.

b. **Set up your Red File** and begin previewing new listings.

c. **Set up 5 Buyer files** with all the paperwork required by your brokerage, your Buyer's Task List, Buyer's Questionnaire and Deal Tracking Form.

## 4. Practice makes Perfect

**Continue practicing to write offers** for different types of properties, using different conditions and terms. Have your broker/ manager check them to make sure they're correct and realistic.

# WEEK 6

## 1. Continue Role Playing & Prospecting Calls

a. Continue your daily role playing sessions.

b. Continue making at least 100 prospecting calls daily.

c. Continue tracking the number of contacts and appointments you make each day.

## 2. Buyers' Presentation

a. Develop your Buyers' Presentation.

b. Rehearse it at least 5 times this week.

c. Role play it consistently with another REALTOR®.

## 3. On the Road Again

a. Download the following items from www.foundationsforsuccess.com:

- Buyers' Questionnaire
- Home Buyer's Scorecard
- "Rules of the Road"

b. Organize your Buyer Showing System.

- Modify the downloaded files as needed and include them in your system.

c. Check with your broker or manager for the specifics of booking showings in your area.

d. **Set up your post-sale Buyer's Service System.**

## 4. Run an Open House this weekend

a. **Download the Open House Checklist from www.foundationsforsuccess.com.**

b. **Choose the day you want to run it.**

c. **Try to schedule it on Monday or Tuesday.**

d. **Follow the checklist for the Open House.**

## 5. Doorknock in Your Farm Area

a. **Doorknock in your farm area at least 3 times this week and track your contacts.**

# WEEK 7

## 1. Continue Role Playing & Prospecting Calls

a. Continue your daily role playing sessions.

b. Continue making 100 prospecting calls daily.

c. Track the number of contacts and appointments you make each day.

d. Track the number of Appointments you make each day. What's your conversion rate?

## 2. Listing Presentation

a. Develop your Listing Presentation.

b. Rehearse it at least 5 times this week.

c. Role play it consistently with another REALTOR®.

d. Develop your Pre-Listing Package

e. Have 10 printed and ready to use.

## 3. Objection Handling

a. Role play your Objection Handling with a colleague for half an hour every day for the following:
   i. Prospecting Calls
   ii. Listing Presentations
   iii. Buyer's Presentations

iv.   Closing for offers with Buyers

## 4. Run an Open House this weekend

Track your Contacts and Appointments using the Contact Tracking Form.

## 5. Doorknock Your Farm Area

**Doorknock in your farm area at least 3 times this week and track your contacts.**

# WEEK 8

## 1. Continue Role Playing & Prospecting Calls

a. **Continue your daily role playing sessions.**

b. **Make 100 prospecting calls daily.**

c. **Track the number of contacts and appointments you make each day.** Review your conversion rate with your broker/manager to help polish your skills.

## 2. Get the Word Out

a. Pick 5 properties from your local real estate magazine.

b. Pull up the listings on your local MLS® System.

c. Using the MLS information and the description in the magazine, rewrite the ads.

d. Use the methods described in Volume 5 to develop ads that focus on creating an emotional draw for potential buyers and have a call to action at the end.

    i. Define the benefits to the buyer of the particular features of the house

    ii. Add an emotional component to the benefits

    iii. What's your Target Market?

    iv. Which of the benefits will attract your target market?

v. Remember to tie the headline, fist line and last line together.

vi. What's your call to action?

## 3. Objection Handling

a. Role play your Objection Handling and Closing skills with a colleague for half an hour every day for the following:

  v. Prospecting Calls

  vi. Listing Presentations

  vii. Buyer's Presentations

  viii. Closing for offers with Buyers

## 4. Run an Open House this weekend

Track your Contacts and Appointments using the Contact Tracking Form and the Weekly Tracker.

## 5. Doorknock Your Farm Area

**Doorknock in your farm area at least 3 times this week and track your contacts.**

# APPENDIX

All forms, charts and checklists contained in this Appendix are also available for download on www.foundationsforsuccess.com.

# APPENDIX

## BUSINESS PLANNING WORKSHEETS

| INCOME GOAL | AVERAGE COMMISSION | TRANSACTIONS NEEDED |
|---|---|---|
| $ _____ | $ _____ | _____ |

Enter the percentage of your business you want to come from Listings and from Buyers.

| LISTINGS | BUYERS |
|---|---|
| % | % |

Calculate the number of total listings and buyers needed to reach your goal.

| TRANSACTIONS NEEDED | PERCENTAGE FROM LISTINGS | PERCENTAGE FROM BUYERS |
|---|---|---|
| | % | % |
| | TOTAL SOLD LISTINGS NEEDED | TOTAL SOLD BUYERS NEEDED |
| | | |

APPENDIX

## Listings

**Enter the number of sold listings needed from above.**

Total Sold Listings needed _____

Average Listings Taken to Listings Sold Ratio   50 – 60%

Your Listings Taken to Listings Sold Ratio _____ %

Total Listings Required _____

Average # of Listing Appointments needed for each
Listing Taken                                   5 - 7

Your # of Listing Appointments needed for
each Listing Taken _____

Number of Listing Appointments needed
(Total Listings needed x # of
appointments/listing) _____

## Purchases

**Enter the number of Sold Buyers required from the chart above.**

Total Buyers Needed _____

Average Written to Close Percentage          75 - 80%

Your Written to Close Percentage _____ %

Number of Written Contracts needed
(Total Buyers needed x Written to Close
ratio) _____

**Enter the number of contacts required for each appointment.**

Averages

| | |
|---|---|
| Contacts needed for each Appointment (1st year) | 120 – 130 |
| 2nd - 5th year | 50 - 60 |
| 6th year + | 30 - 40 |
| Contacts Required per Appointment | |
| Total Appointments Needed (Listing + Buyer Appointments) | |
| Total Yearly Contacts Required | |
| **Total Daily Contacts Required**, Working 225 Days per Year | |

# APPENDIX

Goal: Generate _____ Transactions

| Source of Business | Number of Transactions | Quarterly Target | |
|---|---|---|---|
| Referrals from Past Clients / Sphere of Influence & Repeat Clients | | Q1    Q2 | Q3    Q4 |
| Open Houses | | Q1    Q2 | Q3    Q4 |
| Website / Social Media | | Q1    Q2 | Q3    Q4 |
| Prospecting | | Q1    Q2 | Q3    Q4 |
| Ad / Sign Calls | | Q1    Q2 | Q3    Q4 |
| Other Networking | | Q1    Q2 | Q3    Q4 |
| FSBO / Expireds | | Q1    Q2 | Q3    Q4 |
| Just Listed / Just Sold Marketing | | Q1    Q2 | Q3    Q4 |
| Commercial | | Q1    Q2 | Q3    Q4 |
| Other (Specify) | | Q1    Q2 | Q3    Q4 |

**Quarterly Targets Total**

Q1 - _____    Q2 - _____    Q3 - _____    Q4 - _____

# FOUNDATIONS FOR SUCCESS

## TACTICAL PLAN

**Task –**

| Objective | | Deadline | Achieved |
|---|---|---|---|
| 1 | | | |
| 2 | | | |
| 3 | | | |
| 4 | | | |
| 5 | | | |

**Task –**

| Objective | | Deadline | Achieved |
|---|---|---|---|
| 1 | | | |
| 2 | | | |
| 3 | | | |
| 4 | | | |
| 5 | | | |

# TACTICAL PLAN CONT'D...

| Task – | | Deadline | Achieved |
|---|---|---|---|
| Objective | | | |
| 1 | | | |
| 2 | | | |
| 3 | | | |
| 4 | | | |
| 5 | | | |

| Task – | | Deadline | Achieved |
|---|---|---|---|
| Objective | | | |
| 1 | | | |
| 2 | | | |
| 3 | | | |
| 4 | | | |
| 5 | | | |

# WEEKLY SCHEDULE

| | MONDAY | TUESDAY | WEDNESDAY | THURSDAY | FRIDAY | SATURDAY | SUNDAY |
|---|---|---|---|---|---|---|---|
| 8:00 - 8:30 | | | | | | | |
| 8:30 - 9:00 | | | | | | | |
| 9:00 - 9:30 | | | | | | | |
| 9:30 - 10:00 | | | | | | | |
| 10:00 - 10:30 | | | | | | | |
| 10:30 - 11:00 | | | | | | | |
| 11:00 - 11:30 | | | | | | | |
| 11:30 - 12:00 | | | | | | | |
| 12:00 - 12:30 | | | | | | | |
| 12:30 - 1:00 | | | | | | | |
| 1:00 - 1:30 | | | | | | | |
| 1:30 - 2:00 | | | | | | | |
| 2:00 - 2:30 | | | | | | | |
| 2:30 - 3:00 | | | | | | | |
| 3:00 - 3:30 | | | | | | | |
| 3:30 - 4:00 | | | | | | | |
| 4:00 - 4:30 | | | | | | | |
| 4:30 - 5:00 | | | | | | | |
| 5:00 - 5:30 | | | | | | | |
| 5:30 - 6:00 | | | | | | | |
| 6:00 - 6:30 | | | | | | | |
| 6:30 - 7:00 | | | | | | | |
| 7:00 - 7:30 | | | | | | | |
| 7:30 - 8:00 | | | | | | | |
| 8:00 - 8:30 | | | | | | | |
| 8:30 - 9:00 | | | | | | | |

# APPENDIX

# FOUNDATIONS FOR SUCCESS
## CONTACT TRACKING SHEET

**Daily Target**_____      **Weekly Target** _____

| | | | | | | | | | |
|---|---|---|---|---|---|---|---|---|---|
| 1 | 2 | 3 | 4 | 5 | 6 | 7 | 8 | 9 | 10 |
| 11 | 12 | 13 | 14 | 15 | 16 | 17 | 18 | 19 | 20 |
| 21 | 22 | 23 | 24 | 25 | 26 | 27 | 28 | 29 | 30 |
| 31 | 32 | 33 | 34 | 35 | 36 | 37 | 38 | 39 | 40 |
| 41 | 42 | 43 | 44 | 45 | 46 | 47 | 48 | 49 | 50 |
| 51 | 52 | 53 | 54 | 55 | 56 | 57 | 58 | 59 | 60 |
| 61 | 62 | 63 | 64 | 65 | 66 | 67 | 68 | 69 | 70 |
| 71 | 72 | 73 | 74 | 75 | 76 | 77 | 78 | 79 | 80 |
| 81 | 82 | 83 | 84 | 85 | 86 | 87 | 88 | 89 | 90 |
| 91 | 92 | 93 | 94 | 95 | 96 | 97 | 98 | 99 | 100 |
| 101 | 102 | 103 | 104 | 105 | 106 | 107 | 108 | 109 | 110 |
| 111 | 112 | 113 | 114 | 115 | 116 | 117 | 118 | 119 | 120 |
| 121 | 122 | 123 | 124 | 125 | 126 | 127 | 128 | 129 | 130 |
| 131 | 132 | 133 | 134 | 135 | 136 | 137 | 138 | 139 | 140 |
| 141 | 142 | 143 | 144 | 145 | 146 | 147 | 148 | 149 | 150 |

Place an "X" in box for each contact that doesn't lead to an appointment.

Place an "L" in the box for a Listing Appointment or a "B" for a Buyer's Appointment.

# WEEKLY ACTIVITY TRACKER

| Activity | Mon | Tues | Wed | Thurs | Fri | Sat | Sun | Totals |
|---|---|---|---|---|---|---|---|---|
| Prospecting | | | | | | | | |
| Warm Calls | | | | | | | | |
| Doorknocking | | | | | | | | |
| Pop-bys | | | | | | | | |
| FSBOs | | | | | | | | |
| Open Houses | | | | | | | | |
| Contacts | | | | | | | | |
| Listing Appointments | | | | | | | | |
| Buyer Appointments | | | | | | | | |
| Additions to Database | | | | | | | | |

| Activity | Mon | Tues | Wed | Thurs | Fri | Sat | Sun | Totals |
|---|---|---|---|---|---|---|---|---|
| Prospecting | | | | | | | | |
| Warm Calls | | | | | | | | |
| Doorknocking | | | | | | | | |
| Pop-bys | | | | | | | | |
| FSBOs | | | | | | | | |
| Open Houses | | | | | | | | |
| Contacts | | | | | | | | |
| Listing Appointments | | | | | | | | |
| Buyer Appointments | | | | | | | | |
| Additions to Database | | | | | | | | |

# FOUNDATIONS FOR SUCCESS

## REFERRAL DATABASE QUALIFYING SCRIPT

Hi _____, it's _____.

I was thinking about you the other day and I just thought I'd give you a call and see how everything is going.

I also wanted to let you know that I'm taking a more serious approach to my real estate business and my ultimate goal is to become the person that people think of when they have a real estate question or are thinking about making a move.

I'm calling because when I was reviewing my database I noticed that I'm missing some information. It looks like I'm missing your email addresses / phone numbers / etc. So that we can stay in touch with you, I need to get my records updated, is that okay?"

Great! So let's see, it looks like I need your email address... (Obtain address and ask for any other information needed).

Perfect, thank you! Can I ask you a quick question? If you were thinking about buying or selling a property, or knew anyone who was, would you be comfortable referring them to me?

Yes:   Great.   I send out a free monthly newsletter with information for homeowners and current market statistics. Does this sound like something you might be interested in?

Yes:   Excellent, I'll get you started on my monthly newsletter right away.

No / They know someone they have to refer to: OK. Thanks for your time. If you find that you do need any information, please remember that I'm always available to help. (Eliminate them from your database)

# APPENDIX

One last thing, would you mind if I stayed in touch with you every few months or so to keep you informed of any market changes and of course answer any real estate questions you may have at that time?

That's great.

I look forward to keeping in touch with you. In the meantime, remember, I'm never too busy for any of your referrals and if you have any questions or know of someone thinking of making a move, please feel free to contact me anytime.

# FOUNDATIONS FOR SUCCESS
## <u>REFERRAL DATABASE QUALIFYING SCRIPT WITH APOLOGY</u>

Hi _____, it's _____.

I was thinking about you the other day and I realized we haven't spoken in (quite) a while. I want to apologize for that.

I also wanted to let you know that I'm taking a more serious approach to my real estate business and my ultimate goal is to become the person that people think of when they have a real estate question or are thinking about making a move.

I'm calling because when I was reviewing my database I noticed that I'm missing some information. It looks like I'm missing your email addresses / phone numbers / etc. So that we can stay in touch with you, I need to get my records updated, is that okay?"

Great! So let's see, it looks like I need your email address… (Obtain address and ask for any other information needed).

Perfect, thank you! Can I ask you a quick question? If you were thinking about buying or selling a property, or knew anyone who was, would you be comfortable referring them to me?

Yes: Great. I send out a free monthly newsletter with information for homeowners and current market statistics. Does this sound like something you might be interested in?

Yes: Excellent, I'll get you started on my monthly newsletter right away.


No / They know someone they have to refer to: OK. Thanks for your time. If you find that you do need any information, please remember that I'm always available to help. (Eliminate them from your database)

One last thing, would you mind if I stayed in touch with you every few months or so to keep you informed of any market changes and of course answer any real estate questions you may have at that time?

That's great.

I look forward to keeping in touch with you. In the meantime, remember, I'm never too busy for any of your referrals and if you have any questions or know of someone thinking of making a move, please feel free to contact me anytime.

# FOUNDATIONS FOR SUCCESS

## Monthly Referral Team Marketing Schedule

| Event | Newsletter | Calls | Mini-CMA | Pop-Bys | Cards | Other |
|-------|-----------|-------|----------|---------|-------|-------|
| Jan   |           |       |          |         |       |       |
| Feb   |           |       |          |         |       |       |
| Mar   |           |       |          |         |       |       |
| Apr   |           |       |          |         |       |       |
| May   |           |       |          |         |       |       |
| Jun   |           |       |          |         |       |       |
| Jul   |           |       |          |         |       |       |
| Aug   |           |       |          |         |       |       |
| Sep   |           |       |          |         |       |       |
| Oct   |           |       |          |         |       |       |
| Nov   |           |       |          |         |       |       |
| Dec   |           |       |          |         |       |       |

# LEAD FOLLOW UP TOOLS
# LEAD TRACKING FORM

**TACTICAL LEAD FOLLOW-UP**

| LEAD NAME | DATE OF FIRST CONTACT | |
|---|---|---|
| RES. PHONE | CELL PHONE | DATE OF FIRST CONTACT |
| BUS. PHONE | EMAIL | FOLLOW-UP DATE |

| FOLLOW UP DONE |
|---|

**BUYER**

WANTS:

| | | |
|---|---|---|
| SINGLE FAMILY ☐ | CONDO ☐ | |
| PRICE RANGE: | AREA: | |
| TYPE: | STYLE: | |
| DETACHED ☐ | 2 STOREY ☐ | |
| SEMI DETACHED ☐ | BUNGALOW ☐ | |
| TOWNHOME ☐ | SPLIT ☐ | |
| GARAGE: | BEDROOMS: | |
| | BATHROOMS: | |
| BASEMENT: | OTHER: | |

**SELLER**

NOW:

| | |
|---|---|
| SINGLE FAMILY ☐ | CONDO ☐ |
| STYLE: | BASEMENT: |
| SQ. FT.: | BEDROOMS: |
| BATHS: | GARAGE: |
| | COMMUNITY: |

LEAD SOURCE:

REFERRAL ☐  AD ☐  SIGN ☐  CALL ☐  DK ☐

| THANK YOU NOTE SENT | GIFT SENT |
|---|---|

ADDITIONAL INFO:

## SAMPLE SELLER EMAIL TEMPLATE

Dear Mr. and Mrs. Smith,

Thanks for speaking with me yesterday at our Open House at 123 Cherry Tree Lane.

You expressed an interest in selling your home and I wanted to make sure I followed up and answered any questions you had about that process.

Selling your home can sometimes be a daunting procedure, but it's my job to eliminate the stress and worry from the process. The most important difference in the way I do things is to tailor the services I offer to the specific ways you want them provided, rather than providing the same services to everyone.

Sound intriguing? Then let's connect by Tuesday, so I can demonstrate more about how I can help you get your home sold, in the time frame that best suits you, for more money, with truly personalized, worry-free service. Call me at 123-456-7890 and we can schedule a time.

## SAMPLE BUYER EMAIL TEMPLATE

Dear Mr. and Mrs. Smith,

Thanks for speaking with me yesterday at our Open House at 123 Cherry Tree Lane.

You expressed an interest in buying a new home and I wanted to make sure I followed up and answered any questions you had about that process.

Buying a home can sometimes be a daunting procedure, but it's my job to eliminate the stress and worry from the process. The most important difference in the way I do things is to tailor the services I offer to the specific ways you want them provided, rather than providing the same services to everyone.

Sound intriguing? Then let's connect by Tuesday, so I can demonstrate more about how I can help you find your next home, in the time frame that best suits you, for the best price, with truly personalized, worry-free service. Call me at 123-456-7890 and we can schedule a time.

## SAMPLE SELLER TEXT MESSAGE TEMPLATE

Hi Mr. and Mrs. Smith,

Thanks for speaking with me yesterday at our Open House at 123 Cherry Tree Lane.

I wanted to make sure I followed up and answered any questions you had about selling your home.

It's my job to eliminate the stress and worry from the process by tailoring the services I offer to you, rather than providing the same services to everyone.

Sound intriguing? Then let's connect by Tuesday, so I can demonstrate more about how I can help you get your home sold, in the time frame that best suits you, for more money, with truly personalized, worry-free service. Call me at 123-456-7890 and we can schedule a time.

## SAMPLE BUYER TEXT MESSAGE TEMPLATE

Hi Mr. and Mrs. Smith,

Thanks for speaking with me yesterday at our Open House at 123 Cherry Tree Lane.

I wanted to make sure I followed up and answered any questions you had about buying a new home.

It's my job to eliminate the stress and worry from the process by tailoring the services I offer to you, rather than providing the same services to everyone.

Sound intriguing? Then let's connect by Tuesday, so I can demonstrate more about how I can help you find your next home, in the time frame that best suits you, for the best price, with truly personalized, worry-free service. Call me at 123-456-7890 and we can schedule a time.

## SAMPLE SELLER PHONE CALL MESSAGE SCRIPT

Hi Mr. / Mrs. Smith,

It's _____ with _____ calling. We met yesterday at our Open House at 123 Cherry Tree Lane.

You expressed an interest in selling your home and I wanted to make sure I followed up and answered any questions you had about that process.

I know that selling your home can sometimes be a daunting procedure, but it's my job to eliminate the stress and worry from the process. The most important difference in the way I do things is to tailor the services I offer to the specific ways you want them provided, rather than providing the same services to everyone.

Does that sound intriguing?

Then let's schedule a time when I can demonstrate how I can help you get your home sold, in the time frame that best suits you, for more money, with truly personalized, worry-free service. Call me at 123-456-7890 and we can schedule a time.

# APPENDIX

## SAMPLE BUYER PHONE CALL MESSAGE SCRIPT

Hi Mr. / Mrs. Smith,

It's _____ with _____ calling. We met yesterday at our Open House at 123 Cherry Tree Lane.

You expressed an interest in buying a new home and I wanted to make sure I followed up and answered any questions you had about that process.

I know that buying a home can sometimes be a daunting procedure, but it's my job to eliminate the stress and worry from the process. The most important difference in the way I do things is to tailor the services I offer to the specific ways you want them provided, rather than providing the same services to everyone.

Does that sound intriguing?

Then let's schedule a time when I can demonstrate how I can help you find your next home, in the time frame that best suits you, for the best price, with truly personalized, worry-free service. Call me at 123-456-7890 and we can schedule a time.

# SCRIPTS

# APPENDIX

## Building Rapport

The ability to build rapport, to connect with someone, is vital in successful prospecting. Communication is much more than the ability to talk or listen to someone; it's a combination of verbal and non-verbal components within the conversation. About 55% of communication is non-verbal, which means that when you're speaking to someone on the other end of a phone you've lost 55% of your ability to influence them. So your words, tone, inflection, timing and ability to actively listen are even more important.

Some key points to remember, when speaking on the phone, at someone's door or in a meeting are:

1) Mirror – match the other person's speech patterns and body language. If they're speaking quickly or loudly, you must speak quickly or loudly. If they're standing with their arms crossed, match them. This technique increases the other person's sense that you're "in tune" with them.

2) Actively Listen – There's an old saying that God gave us two ears and one mouth so that we can listen twice as much as we talk. Active listening is the skill of being able to listen to what the other person means, rather than what they're saying.

   a. Start by asking a Question and then Listen
      Most of us try to decide what the other person is saying and come up with a response before the other person is finished speaking. This creates a barrier to our ability to truly hear the meaning behind what the person is saying and creates a more confrontational approach to the conversation. "They're saying this, so I'll need to say that."

b.  Repeat the Answer back to them

A large part of active listening is to confirm with the other person that what you're hearing is actually what they're saying. "So, what I'm hearing you say is… Is that right?"

c.  Express Your Understanding

Confirming that you understand their point of view, even if you disagree with it, eliminates the possibility of the conversation becoming confrontational.

3) Find Common Ground – People want to deal with like-minded people. Try to find something that will allow you to establish a connection to the other person, like kids, a dog, a similar hobby, etc. This will help the other person become more comfortable with you and establish a mutual connection.

4) Be Honest And Authentic – Don't try to be someone you're not. Always be yourself and answer any questions honestly. People can sense when someone is trying to be someone they're not or is lying and this will eliminate any trust or connection that may have been built to this point. If you don't know an answer, tell them and then find out later.

5) Provide Value – Jim Rohn said that "Giving is better than receiving because giving starts the receiving process." Providing the other person with something of value to them demonstrates that you're focussing on their interests, rather than yours and begins the process of building trust and respect. When answering an ad or sign call, give the other

person the answer they're looking for, but remember to ask them for something in return.

6) Always Follow a Script or a Guide - Having a specific dialogue / script prepared and rehearsed reduces the opportunity of getting drawn off track or "stepping on your tongue". Any script should be thoroughly rehearsed. It should become part of your natural cadence and conversational style.

7) Practice – The only way for a script to truly become your own is to rehearse it over and over. And the only way to make it perfect is to make sure you get it right each time you rehearse. Vince Lombardi said "Practice does not make perfect. Only perfect practice makes perfect."

## **RESPONSES TO ANTICIPATED OBJECTIONS**

1.  No Interest in You or Your Offer

    _____

    _____

    _____

    _____

    _____

    _____

2.  No Authority to Act

    _____

    _____

    _____

    _____

    _____

    _____

3.  No Need

    _____

    _____

    _____

    _____

    _____

4.  No Time

    _____

    _____

    _____

    _____

5. Previous Bad Experience

_____
_____
_____
_____
_____
_____

6. Likes the Competition

_____
_____
_____
_____
_____

7. Wants Lower Commission

_____
_____
_____
_____
_____

8. Family Member / Friend in the Business

_____
_____
_____
_____
_____

# APPENDIX

## PHONE PROSPECTING SCRIPTS

### General Approach

You:    "Hello Mr./Miss/Ms./Mrs._____. My name is _____ with XYZ Realty.

"I just want to let you know that I'll be really brief. The reason I'm calling today is that I wanted to get a chance to speak to people about the real estate market in the area. I'm sure you've heard that it's a hot market right now. I was wondering if you had any questions about the market?

Prospect: No.

You:    OK. Can I ask how long you've lived there?

Prospect: 10 years

You:    (engage them – ask questions)

OK.    I was wondering if you know what your home is worth in this market.

Prospect: We think it's worth $_____. /  No.

You:    OK. Would it be helpful if I came out and took a look at it and gave you a better idea of what homes are selling for in the area and what your home is worth?

Yes:    OK. How would _____am/pm tomorrow would work for you, or would _____am/pm on _____ work better?

No:    OK. I'd like to ask whether you are thinking about moving in the near future." (Y/N)

Yes: OK. (Qualify them – open ended questions. Close for appointment)

No: Do you know of anyone who may be? (Y/N)

Yes: Would you be able to give me their name and perhaps their number and I'll give them a call to follow up.

No: And you're definitely not thinking about it?

No: Can I ask you one last question? If you were thinking about buying or selling, or knew anyone who was, do you have a REALTOR® that you'd work with?

Yes: OK. Thanks for your time.

No: Well, you know, I'd love to be that REALTOR®. Would it be alright if I sent you some information about who I am and what I do and then follow up in a few days to see if you have any questions?

Yes: OK. May I have your email address and I'll get that out to you right away. Thanks again.

No: OK. Thanks again.

## Just Listed Approach

You: "Hello Mr./Miss/Ms./Mrs._____. My name
is _____ with XYZ Realty.

"I just want to let you know that I'll be really brief. The
reason I'm calling today is that we just listed a home (a
home was just listed) in your neighbourhood. It's listed at
$_____ and there's a real demand for homes in
your area right now. I was wondering if you had any
questions about the market in your area / neighbourhood.
(Answer their questions if they have any.)

Prospect: No.

You: OK. Can I ask how long you've lived there?

Prospect: We've been here _____

You: OK. I was wondering if you know what your home is
worth in this market.

Prospect: We think it's worth $_____.

You: OK. Would it be helpful if I came out and took a look at
it and gave you a better idea of what homes are selling for
in the area and what your home is worth?

Yes: Great. How would _____am/pm tomorrow work for you,
or would _____am/pm on _____ work
better?

No: OK. Thanks. Can I ask you one last question? If you were
thinking about buying or selling, or knew anyone who was,
do you have a REALTOR® that you'd work with?

Yes: OK. Thanks for your time.

No:     Well, you know, I'd love to be that REALTOR®. Would it be alright if I sent you some information about who I am and what I do and then follow up in a few days to see if you have any questions?

Yes:    Great. Would you prefer it by mail or email?

OK. Thanks again.

## Just Sold Approach

You: "Hello Mr./Miss/Ms./Mrs._____. My name is _____ with XYZ Realty.

"I just want to let you know that I'll be really brief. The reason I'm calling today is that we just sold a home (a home was just sold) in your neighbourhood. It sold at _____% of asking in _____ days. There's a real demand for homes in your area right now and I was wondering if you had any questions about the market in your area / neighbourhood. Answer their questions if they have any.

Prospect: No.

You: OK. Can I ask how long you've lived there?

Prospect: We've been here _____

You: OK. I was wondering if you know what your home is worth in this market.

Prospect: We think it's worth $_____. / No.

You: OK. Would it be helpful if I came out and took a look at it and gave you a better idea of what homes are selling for in the area and what your home is worth?

Yes: Great. How would _____am/pm tomorrow work for you, or would _____am/pm on _____ work better?

No: OK. Thanks. Can I ask you one last question? If you were thinking about buying or selling, or knew anyone who was, do you have a REALTOR® that you'd work with?

Yes: OK. Thanks for your time.

No: Well, you know, I'd love to be that REALTOR®. Would it be alright if I sent you some information about who I am and what I do and then follow up in a few days to see if you have any questions?

Yes: Great. Would you prefer it by mail or email?

No: OK. Thanks again.

## Buyer Specific Approach

You: "Hello Mr./Miss/Ms./Mrs._____. My name is _____ with XYZ Realty.

"I just want to let you know that I'll be really brief. The reason I'm calling today is that I'm working with a family who's really interested in buying a home in your neighbourhood. I'd like to ask whether you are thinking about moving in the near future." (Y/N)

Yes: OK. (Qualify them – open ended questions. Close for appointment)

No: If I could get you a price that you'd be happy with, would you consider selling to them?

Yes: Great. (Qualify them – open ended questions. Close for appointment)

No: Thanks for considering it. Do you know of anyone who may be? (Y/N)

Yes: Would you be able to give me their name and perhaps their number and I'll give them a call to follow up.

No: And you're definitely not thinking about it?

No: OK. Thanks. Can I ask you one last question? If you were thinking about buying or selling, or knew anyone who was, do you have a REALTOR® that you'd work with?

Yes: OK. Thanks for your time.

No: Well, you know, I'd love to be that REALTOR®. Would it be alright if I sent you some information about who I am and what I do and then follow up in a few days to see if you have any questions?

Yes:   Great. Would you prefer it by mail or email?

No:   OK. Thanks again.

Yes:   OK. May I have your email address and I'll get that out to you right away. Thanks again.

No:   OK. Thanks again.

## DOORKNOCKING SCRIPTS

### General Approach

You:    Good morning / afternoon. My name is _____ with XYZ Realty.

I'm working in your neighbourhood and wanted to make sure I introduced myself. As the neighbourhood professional I like to make sure I keep up to speed on everything that's going on. Here are the latest stats for this community (Hand them the Area Market Update).

I was wondering if you have any questions about the real estate market?

Them:   Yes. (Answer their questions as completely as possible. You want to demonstrate that you're the person they want to deal with.)

No: OK. Can I ask how long you've lived there?

Prospect:  We've been here _____

You:    OK. *(Engage them in a conversation about the community – Build Rapport)*

I was wondering if you know what your home is worth in this market.

Prospect:  We think it's worth $_____. / No.

You:    OK. Would it be helpful if I came out and took a look at it and gave you a better idea of what homes are selling for in the area and what your home is worth?

Yes: Great. How would _____am/pm tomorrow work for you, or would _____am/pm on _____ work better?

No: OK. Thanks. Can I ask you one last question? If you were thinking about buying or selling, or knew anyone who was, do you have a REALTOR® that you'd work with?

Yes: OK. Thanks for your time.

No: Well, you know, I'd love to be that REALTOR®. Would it be alright if I sent you some information about who I am and what I do and then follow up in a few days to see if you have any questions?

Yes: Great. Would you prefer it by mail or email?

No: OK. Thanks. Just before I go, I send a monthly Area Market Update to quite a few people in the area and was wondering if you'd be interested in receiving it, with no obligation? (Y/N)

Yes: OK. May I have your email address and I'll get that out to you right away. By the way, do you know of anyone who may be thinking about moving in the near future? (Y/N)

Yes: Would you be able to give me their name and perhaps their number and I'll give them a call to follow up?

No: And you're definitely not thinking about it? *No.* OK. Thanks again.

## Just Listed Approach

You:   Hi, my name is _____ with XYZ Realty.

I just want to let you know that I'll be really brief. The reason I'm here today is to let you know that 123 Anywhere Street just listed at $_____ and there's a real demand for homes in your area right now. I was wondering if you have any questions about the real estate market?

Them:  Yes. (Answer their questions as completely as possible. You want to demonstrate that you're the person they want to deal with.)

No: OK. Can I ask how long you've lived there?

Prospect: We've been here _____

You:   OK. *(Engage them in a conversation about the community – Build Rapport)*

I was wondering if you know what your home is worth in this market.

Prospect: We think it's worth $_____.

You:   OK. Would it be helpful if I took a look at it and gave you a better idea of what homes are selling for in the area and what your home is worth?

Yes:  OK. How would _____am/pm tomorrow would work for you, or would _____am/pm on _____ work better?

No: OK. Thanks. Can I ask you one last question? If you were thinking about buying or selling, or knew anyone who was, do you have a REALTOR® that you'd work with?

Yes: OK. Thanks for your time.

No: Well, you know, I'd love to be that REALTOR®. Would it be alright if I sent you some information about who I am and what I do and then follow up in a few days to see if you have any questions?

Yes: Great. Would you prefer it by mail or email?

No: OK. Thanks. Just before I go, I send a monthly Area Market Update to quite a few people in the area and was wondering if you'd be interested in receiving it, with no obligation? (Y/N)

Yes: OK. May I have your email address and I'll get that out to you right away. By the way, do you know of anyone who may be thinking about moving in the near future? (Y/N)

Yes: Would you be able to give me their name and perhaps their number and I'll give them a call to follow up?

No: And you're definitely not thinking about it? *No.* OK. Thanks again.

## Just Sold Approach

You: Hi, my name is _____ with XYZ REALTY.

I just want to let you know that I'll be really brief. The reason I'm here today is to let you know that 123 Anywhere Street just sold at _____% of asking, in _____ days. There's a real demand for homes in your area right now and I was wondering if you have any questions about the real estate market?

Them: Yes. (Answer their questions as completely as possible. You want to demonstrate that you're the person they want to deal with.)

No: OK. Can I ask how long you've lived there?

Prospect: We've been here _____

You: OK. *(Engage them in a conversation about the community – Build Rapport)*

I was wondering if you know what your home is worth in this market.

Prospect: We think it's worth $_____.

You: OK. Would it be helpful if I took a look at it and gave you a better idea of what homes are selling for in the area and what your home is worth?

Yes: OK. How would _____am/pm tomorrow would work for you, or would _____am/pm on _____ work better?

No: OK. Thanks. Can I ask you one last question? If you were thinking about buying or selling, or knew anyone who was, do you have a REALTOR® that you'd work with?

Yes: OK. Thanks for your time.

No: Well, you know, I'd love to be that REALTOR®. Would it be alright if I sent you some information about who I am and what I do and then follow up in a few days to see if you have any questions?

Yes: Great. Would you prefer it by mail or email?

No: OK. Thanks. Just before I go, I send a monthly Area Market Update to quite a few people in the area and was wondering if you'd be interested in receiving it, with no obligation? (Y/N)

Yes: OK. May I have your email address and I'll get that out to you right away. By the way, do you know of anyone who may be thinking about moving in the near future? (Y/N)

Yes: Would you be able to give me their name and perhaps their number and I'll give them a call to follow up?

No: And you're definitely not thinking about it? *No.* OK. Thanks again.

## Buyer Specific Approach

You:    Hi, my name is _____ with XYZ Realty.

        I just want to let you know that I'll be really brief. The reason I'm here today is that I'm working with a family who's really interested in buying a home in your neighbourhood. I'd like to ask whether you are thinking about moving in the near future." (Y/N)

Yes:    OK. (Qualify them – open ended questions. Close for appointment)

No:    If I could get you a price that you'd be happy with, would you consider selling to them?

Yes:    Great. (Qualify them – open ended questions. Close for appointment)

No:    Thanks for considering it. Do you know of anyone who may be? (Y/N)

Yes:    Would you be able to give me their name and perhaps their number and I'll give them a call to follow up.

No:    And you're definitely not thinking about it?

No:    OK. Thanks. Can I ask you one last question? If you were thinking about buying or selling, or knew anyone who was, do you have a REALTOR® that you'd work with?

Yes:    OK. Thanks for your time.

No:    Well, you know, I'd love to be that REALTOR®. Would it be alright if I sent you some information about who I am and what I do and then follow up in a few days to see if you have any questions?

Yes:  Great.  Would you prefer it by mail or email?

No:  OK.  Thanks again.

Yes:  OK.  May I have your email address and I'll get that out to you right away.  Thanks again.

No:  OK.  Thanks again.

## SAMPLE QUALIFYING QUESTIONS FOR AD / SIGN CALL

How long have you been looking?

When do you want to move / How soon do you want to be in your new property?

Why are you thinking of buying?

If you could design the ideal moving situation for your family, what would it look like?

Have you seen anything you really like?

Do you need to sell your current home before you can buy?   Is your home currently on the market?

Have you bought a property in the past?

Have you met with a lender yet? What Price Range are you looking in?

When can we meet to discuss your property search?

Are you working with another agent?

What can I do to make it easier for you to get the kind of real estate information you are looking for?

Tell me the process you typically use to make decisions like this?

What is the most important service you want from a real estate agent like myself?

Besides that, what's next? (Go 3 deep)

## AD/SIGN CALL SCRIPTS

The secret to success when dealing with ad or sign calls is to engage the caller, build rapport and avoid giving them all the information they want all at once. The whole purpose is to **close the caller for a face to face appointment** rather than just meeting them and showing them the property they're calling about.

### Inbound Calls

You:     Hello, _____ speaking. May I help you?

Them:   I'm calling about your ad in the paper...

You:     Great, thanks for calling. Can you tell me a little bit about which property you're calling about? Oh, by the way, just in case we get cut off, can I get your name and number so I can call you back?

*They give you their name and number.*

You:     Thanks. Now, which home were you calling about?

Them:   The two storey with four bedrooms and three baths.

You:     Oh yes, that's a great house. What would you like to know about it?

Them:   I'd like to know where it is and the price.

You:     It's in the _____ area of _____. Is that an area you're interested in? (Where)

Them:   It's one of the areas we're thinking about... Yes...Not really...

You:     OK. What other areas were you thinking about? (Where)

Them:   *lists several*

You:   How soon where you thinking of moving? (When)

Them:   When we find the right place... When we sell our other house... Very shortly.....

You:   And what kind of price range are you looking in? (How much)

Them:   *provides a price range*

You:   Unfortunately, that house isn't in that price range. But I have several homes in those areas that are. Would you like to hear about some of them? (Use Red File)

***(or)***

OK, well that house is listed at $_____. Would that work for you?

Them:   Yes it would.

You:   Great. Let me tell you a little about the home. *(Describe the home for them)* Does that sound like what you're looking for?

1)

Them:   Yes.

You:   OK. Why don't we get together and I can show it to you? Would _____ at _____ work for you or is _____ at _____ better?

2)

Them:   No.

You:    OK. So that's not what you're looking for. Would you like to hear about some of the other properties that are available in the same area and price range?

Them:   Sure.

You:    *Read the remarks from 2 listings.* Do any of those sound interesting?

Them:   Yes...I like the one...

You:    Great. Why don't we get together and I can show it/them to you? Would _____ at _____ work for you or is _____ at _____ better?

## Outbound Calls

You:    Hi _____, this is _____ from _____ calling. You called me looking for some information on a home that I have advertised. How can I help you?

Them:   I'm calling about the two storey with four bedrooms and three baths.

You:    Oh yes, that's a great house. What would you like to know about it?

Them:   I'd like to know where it is and the price.

You:    It's in the _____ area of _____. Is that an area you're interested in? (Where)

Them:   It's one of the areas we're thinking about... Yes...Not really...

You:    OK. What other areas were you thinking about? (Where)

Them: *lists several*

You: How soon where you thinking of moving? (When)

Them: When we find the right place... When we sell our other house... Very shortly.....

You: And what kind of price range are you looking in? (How much)

Them: *provides a price range*

You: Unfortunately, that house isn't in that price range. But I have several homes in those areas that are. Would you like to hear about some of them? (Use Red File)

*(or)*

OK, well that house is listed at $_____. Would that work for you?

Them: Yes it would.

You: Great. Let me tell you a little about the home. *(Describe the home for them)* Does that sound like what you're looking for?

1)

Them: Yes.

You: OK. Why don't we get together and I can show it to you? Would _____ at _____ work for you or is _____ at _____ better?

2)

Them: No.

You:     OK. So that's not what you're looking for. Would you like to hear about some of the other properties that are available in the same area and price range?

Them:    Sure.

You:     *Read the remarks from 2 listings.* Do any of those sound interesting?

Them:    Yes…I like the one…

You:     Great. Why don't we get together and I can show it/them to you? Would _____ at _____ work for you or is _____ at _____ better?

## OBJECTION HANDLING

## AD / SIGN CALL OBJECTIONS

### CAN YOU GIVE ME THE ADDRESS

Them:   I just want the address. We want to drive by and take a look and then we'll get back to you.

You:   OK. I understand how you feel. A lot of people feel the same. But what I've found is that just driving by doesn't give you the real feel of the house. Let me ask you, when you bought your current place, did you buy it because of how it looked outside, or how you felt when you were in it?

*Most people will reply that it was how they felt when they were inside. Except investors.*

You:   OK, so wouldn't it make sense to take a look at the interior of this house to see if it's the right feel?

1)

Them:   Yeah, I guess so.

You:   OK. I'm free at _____ today, or would _____ work better for you? And while we're out, I'll set up a couple of other places for you to see. How does that sound? *(Make sure both buyers will be available)*

Them:   Sure.

You:   *Confirm time, address and contact info.*

2)

Them:   Maybe, but I'd just like the address.

You: OK. It's _____. *(It's OK to give them the address of your listing)* Would you like to hear about some of the other properties that are available in the same area and price range?

Them: Sure. (Read the remarks from 2 listings)

You: Do any of those sound interesting?

Them: Yes. Could I get the addresses of those as well?

You: Can I ask you a quick question? Is this the neighbourhood you want to be in?

Them: Yes

You: Great. So can you tell a bit more about why you feel driving by the home will help you make a decision? *(They just want to see what it looks like).*

I understand. But I only give out those addresses to my clients. I'd be happy to arrange a time for us to meet to discuss how I can help you find a home, if you're interested and then I can show you the homes that meet your needs. Would today at _____ or tomorrow at _____ work best for you?

## *I JUST WANT TO SEE THE HOUSE*

You: I can understand that, a lot of people I've spoken to feel that way and I'd be happy to show you the home. But what I've found is that when we show someone a home, it's rarely the home they're looking for.

Would you agree that we don't want to waste time looking at homes that aren't what you want?

Them: That makes sense.

In order to do that, I'd suggest we get together and I can find out exactly what it is you're looking for in your new home. I also want to make sure that you're completely up to date on what's happening in the real estate market. That way you can make the best decision when you decide to purchase. Would that be helpful?

Them: That sounds OK.

You: Great. It usually takes about 20 or 30 minutes. Why don't we meet and go over it? How does _____ today sound, or would _____ tomorrow work better for you?

If the Buyer is still insisting on only seeing that home

You: OK. I understand. Unfortunately, my sellers have asked me not to bring anybody through the home without making sure they're qualified to buy it. I'm sure you can understand their concern for safety and that they don't want waste their time with anyone who's not able to buy it.

Buyer: Yes, I can understand that.

You: Great. I can still show you the home, but in order to do that, we'll need to meet for about 20 minutes first. How does _____ today sound, or would _____ tomorrow work better for you?

## CAN YOU JUST EMAIL ME THE INFORMATION ON THE HOME?

You:   I can certainly do that, but let me ask you; are you already getting listings emailed from other agents?

Buyer: I'm working with a couple of other agents and they're sending me listings.

You:   OK. And are you looking in the same areas with all of them?

Buyer: Yes

You:   Let me ask you, have you noticed that the homes they're sending are the same ones?

Them:  Yes.

You:   Here's why. All agents have access to the same information through the MLS system. So the agents you've spoken with have taken what you've told them and plugged that into their system. As a result, they're sending you the same information.

Now, here's how I work. In order to make sure we're not wasting your time or sending you repeats of the same listings, I'd suggest we get together and I can find out exactly what it is you're looking for in your new home. I also want to make sure that you're completely up to date on what's happening in the real estate market. That way you can make the best decision when you decide to purchase. Would that be helpful?

Buyer: That makes sense.

You:   Great. It usually takes about 20 or 30 minutes. Why don't we meet and go over it? How does _____ today sound, or would _____ tomorrow work better for you?

## *WE'RE JUST STARTING THE PROCESS AND NOT SURE WHAT WE'RE LOOKING FOR.*

You: That's great. You know, I can help with that. Why don't I send you my Informed Buyer Guide? It's got great information on what steps are most important when buying a home. Would you like me to send it to you?

Them: Yes

You: Great! What address should I send it to? I'll also follow up on _____ at _____ to make sure you received it.

Do you mind me asking if you've been preapproved for a mortgage yet?

I strongly recommend this as your first step before you begin looking for a home. That way you'll know how much you can spend and won't waste your time or get frustrated looking at homes you can't afford.

Knowing everything is in order will also make it easier when it comes to negotiating. Best of all, if interest rates rise, you'll get the benefit of having locked in at a lower rate.

So, why don't we set up a time to get together so that we can discuss what you're looking for in your next home? That usually takes about 20 or 30 minutes. How does _____ today sound, or would _____ tomorrow work better for you?

## *WE ONLY WANT TO WORK WITH THE LISTING AGENT*

You:   Do you mind me asking why?

Buyer: We can get a better deal by buying through the listing agent because they can reduce their commission.

You:   You know _____, I've heard that a lot, and you're right, some agents may offer to reduce their commission to get the home sold. However, may I explain why that strategy can actually work as a disadvantage?

Buyer: Sure

You:   When an agent lists a home, they have a legal obligation to work in the seller's best interest at all times. This means that the listing agent isn't allowed to disclose any market information that would be harmful to the seller.

That means that if you decide to buy through them, their first obligation is to the seller and not you.

Would you agree that it's impossible to try to get the highest price for one party while at the same time trying to get the lowest price for the other person?

Buyer: That makes sense.

You:   That means that even if they have you under contract as a buyer, they can't negotiate for your best price, while trying to get the top dollar for the seller. Do you see what I mean?

Buyer: Yes

You:   So it only makes sense to have someone working for you, who's committed to acting in your best interests, doesn't it?

Buyer: Yes

You: So, when I work with buyers, my job is to find them the right house at the right price and to work only for you, and your best interests.

Why don't we get together and I can show you how I work. Would that be of interest to you?

Great. I'm available _____ and _____, do one of those work for you?

## *ANOTHER AGENT IS WILLING TO GIVE US PART OF THEIR COMMISSION*

You:   I understand that every dollar counts for you. But, can I tell you why that concerns me?

If the other agent isn't able to stand up for themselves when it comes to negotiating their own salary, how strong do you feel they can possibly be when it comes to negotiating the price of your home against an experienced agent?

I have that strength and the strong negotiating skills so you can rest easy knowing I'll get you the best purchase price possible.

Why don't we get together and go over the value I can bring to your home purchase?

Excellent, I have an opening in my schedule _____ or _____, which would you prefer?

# FOUNDATIONS FOR SUCCESS

Develop your own objection handling using the examples above.

I just want to drive by it. Can you give me the address?

_____

_____

_____

_____

_____

_____

Are you the listing agent? I only look at homes with the listing agent.

_____

_____

_____

_____

_____

_____

Can you just email the information on the home / on what's available?

_____

_____

_____

_____

_____

_____

# APPENDIX

We're just starting the process and not sure what we're looking for.

_____

_____

_____

_____

_____

_____

I want to wait because I think the market will go down.

_____

_____

_____

_____

_____

_____

## BUYER OBJECTIONS

In order to make objection handling less complicated, I've broken down the steps in managing the most common buyer objections into two categories; basic and advanced. The basic skill level utilizes tried and true stock answers that are easily learned. These can be used while practicing and improving your skills using the advanced techniques.

### *WE THINK IT'S OVERPRICED / WE WANT TO GO IN LOWER*

You: OK. I can appreciate that. If you were going to write an offer, what price would you like to pay for the home? ....

Once they give you a price, you have to decide if it's reasonable or unreasonable as a starting point.

You: OK. But I need to explain that at that price we should expect a counteroffer, so my question is, do you absolutely want to buy this home?

Buyer: Yes we do.

You: OK. So in order to make sure you get the home you want at a price you're comfortable with, what I've found is that if we take a closer look at the comparable properties that have sold, it may help you to understand why they're at that asking price. Would that help you?

Buyer: Yes.

Review the comparables to help them better understand why the home is priced where it is.

You: So, now that we've taken a closer look at the properties that have sold in the area, does that help you better understand their pricing?

Buyer: Yes.

Close for the purchase.

**SHARP ANGLE CLOSING QUESTION** - Financing concern

"If I could show you how you could still get this home, and pay a very minimal amount more for it, would that help you make a decision?"

**FEEL, FELT, FOUND** - Financing concern

"What I've found is that by helping you understand how you can still get this home by paying a very minimal amount more for it, it might help you make a more informed decision. Would that help?"

Demonstrate how; "Let's say you pay the additional $20,000 for this house. How long do you expect to live here? (5 years)

At 3% interest that's $4,300 per year, right? That works out to $82 per week or $12 a day. You really like this home, am I right? You want to move, right? Can you afford an extra $12 a day to get the home you want, now?"

## WE WANT TO WAIT. WE THINK THAT PRICES ARE GOING TO DROP

### SHARP ANGLE CLOSING QUESTION

You:    "If I could show you that by waiting for the market to drop, you could actually end up in a position where it costs you more, would that make it easier for you to make a decision about buying this house?"

### FEEL, FELT, FOUND

You:    "I understand how you feel. A lot of my clients have felt that way. But what I've found is that by waiting for the market to drop, you could actually end up in a position where it costs you more. If I could show you how, would that make it easier for you to make a decision about buying this house?"

Buyer: Yes.

Use the latest market trends, stats and demonstrate to them that that, overall, housing prices tend to increase over time.

## *WE WANT TO THINK ABOUT IT*

Them: "We need to talk to our parents about it."…"We like to take our time to think things over."

You: "Buying a house is a big deal and I understand that you would want to think about it. Let me ask you this, you like the house, right? It has what you're looking for, doesn't it?

OK. So, what is it about the purchase that concerns you?"

"So you're not sure about (concern) is that right?"

### *SHARP ANGLE CLOSING QUESTION*

"If we take some time to discuss what you like and don't like about this house, would that help clear things up for you?"

### *FEEL, FELT, FOUND*

"What I've found is that if we take some time to discuss what you like and don't like about the house, it'll help clear things up for you. Would that help?"

Review their Pain / Fear. Why are they making the move? What's their concern? Is the pain of staying greater than their concern about the move?

## *THE HOME IS RUN DOWN*

### *SHARP ANGLE CLOSING QUESTION*

"I understand. But, this home offers you a chance to add your own personal touches. If we took a look at what it might cost to bring it up to your standards, compared with the cost of buying a renovated home, would that help you make a decision?"

### *FEEL, FELT, FOUND*

"What I've found is that if we look at what the cost would be to renovate, compared with the price of a renovated home, it might help you make a decision. Would that help?"

Review their Motivation. Compare their needs and wants to the available homes and their budget.

## *WHAT'S YOUR COMMISSION? (OVER THE PHONE / AT THE DOOR)*

Reply #1.

You: "Mr. / Mrs. Seller, that's a great question. That's one of the first things we'll talk about when I see you. While I understand that you need to know the answer to that, at the same time let me ask you, if you're like most people I talk to, isn't the most important question how much you're going to net on the sale of your property? I'll cover my marketing plan, the timing of your move, my fees, everything you need to know to make the right decision. How does that sound? Why don't we get together to discuss it _____ at _____?"

Reply #2.

You: "That's a great question Mr. / Mrs. Seller. I don't charge a commission unless I sell your home. Why don't we get together so I can see your home and then let's decide on the commission amount after we've talked about what marketing's required to get your home sold for the most amount of money."

Them: But can't you just tell me what percent you charge?

You: "Not really – not until I see your home and we decide what marketing I'm going to do. I can tell you one thing though, before I ask you to sign a contract, I assure you that you will be very satisfied. Fair enough? (Alright) Great, how's _____ at _____?"

### HOW MUCH DO YOU THINK MY HOME'S WORTH? (OVER THE PHONE / AT THE DOOR)

You: "Mr. / Mrs. Seller, that's a great question and one I'm sure you'd want a really accurate answer to. Without having a chance to take a look at your home, it would be unprofessional of me to give you an opinion of its market value. Why don't we set up a time for us to get together so I can take a look through your home and then we can compare it to the other homes that are for sale and have sold in the area? That way I can give you a realistic, accurate figure. How would _____ at _____ work for you?"

Them: But you're supposed to be the neighbourhood expert, right. So can't you just give me an idea of what I could get?)

You:  "Well, I could let you know what the average house is selling for in the area, but your house isn't average is it? Would you say your home has different features than the other homes in the area? What about the things you've done to make it home? I'd have to make some adjustments to the average price and I can't do that without seeing your home. Let's set up a time for me to take a look and then discuss what it's worth. Would _____ at _____ work for you?"

# APPENDIX

## LISTING APPOINTMENT OBJECTIONS

### *I WANT TO FIND A HOUSE BEFORE I PUT MINE ON THE MARKET*

Reply #1

"I understand, finding your new home is important. The concern that I have is that it may take a while to sell your home and then another month to close. Any home you find may be sold before you get yours sold.

What I'd recommend is that we get your home listed and then, when we have an offer on it, we can find your next one. Does that make sense? Why don't we get the paperwork going so I can help you make your move?"

Reply #2

"I understand your concern. I've brought you a list of current listings that fit your needs. Check these out and we will start looking. Once we have this house listed, we can find you the home you're looking for. That way we can close both homes on the same day and you only have to make one move. How does that sound?"

Reply #3

"I understand. We have some options that might help. Once we've got your home on the market, we'll start looking at homes. When we get an offer on yours we can do a couple of things. The first is to set a longer closing date so we have time to continue looking or we can include a condition that ensures that you find a suitable home within a specific time period. How does that sound?"

## *WE WANT A HIGHER LIST PRICE....*

Reply #1

"I understand. Let me ask you this, do you have any questions about the Comparative Analysis I've shown you? You understand that the price range I've recommended is based on the prices that people are paying for homes like yours in this area, right? You've seen the prices of the homes that didn't sell, and remember, houses sell because of price. So, if I can show you how pricing your home higher than the price range I've recommended could actually cost you money as well as valuable time, would you be willing to set a price for your home that reflects what the market is paying?"

Reply #2

"I understand that you want to leave room for negotiation. What I've found is that when people try that, it can create some problems. Can I explain?

First, people decide which homes they want to look at based on price. So if your home is priced above the market, many people will not even consider it for two reasons; it may be above the price range they want, but, even more importantly, buyers nowadays are very savvy. They know the prices in the area where they're looking and won't even consider a home that they feel is overpriced.

So, what does this mean to you? If we price your home out of the market range, we reduce the number of buyers just looking at your home, meaning that there's less of a chance of getting an offer and a higher chance of not getting one for an extended period. That could result, if we do get an offer, in it likely being somewhere at the lower end of the price range.

That means you'd have the potential for ending up with less and taking longer to sell than if we price it properly right out of the gate.

So, doesn't it make more sense to price it properly, get it sold in a better time frame and for more money by listing it within the range we've discussed?"

## ANOTHER AGENT SAID THEY COULD SELL IT FOR MORE MONEY

Reply #1

"I understand your concern. It's kind of confusing isn't it? I mean, you interview four agents and you get four different prices ... right?

Well, here's why. There's a big difference in the way that I operate and the way that a lot of agents operate. Most agents manipulate the stats to show figures that they think you want to hear, because they're desperate to get your listing. Getting your listing makes them feel like they are accomplishing something. That's why they'll tell you whatever price they think you want to hear.

However, I believe that I'm doing both you and me a disservice by listing a home above market price. First, I believe that when I list your home, we've started building a relationship and I don't want to start that relationship off with a lie. Secondly, as your agent, my main goal is to help you achieve your goals, one of which is getting your home sold so you can move onward. So why don't we review the numbers and let's get your home listed at a price that's going to achieve your goals."

Reply #2

"I understand your concern. Did you know that only ___% (currently 56%) of the homes that are listed for sale actually sell?

That's because the other _____% are overpriced. And that happens because some agents are so concerned about just getting a listing that they'll take any listing and they don't care about the seller.

There are three real comparables to understand in the real estate market. The first is the currently listed homes. The second is the homes that have sold in the area. And the third are the homes that haven't sold because they were overpriced, the expireds. The first can also be called the "Wish list" because that what people hope to get. The second is the reality; that's what buyers are prepared to pay for similar homes. And the third is what I call no-man's land. That's where overpriced listings go after they've sat on the market until the contract expires.

So you can list your home to sell, or list it to sit. Why don't we list it at the right price and get you moving?"

Reply #3

"I understand your concern. Of course you want to sell it for the best amount you possibly can and that makes perfect sense.

Let me ask you this. If the other agents told you that once you'd listed your home with them, that you'd have blue skies every day until it sold, would you believe them?

Of course not. That's impossible. Well, it's the same as promising that your house will sell above what the market says it will. It's impossible to predict. So, why don't we review the numbers and let's get your home listed at a price that's going to get it sold."

## THEY CAN ALWAYS MAKE AN OFFER / WE WANT TO TRY IT HIGH FOR A COUPLE OF WEEKS

"I understand that you want to leave room for negotiation. What I've found is that when people try that, it can create some problems. Can I explain?

First, people decide which homes they want to look at based on price. So if your home is priced above the market, many people will not even consider it for two reasons; it may be above the price range they want, but, even more importantly, buyers nowadays are very savvy. They know the prices in the area where they're looking and won't even consider a home that they feel is overpriced.

So, what does this mean to you? If we price your home out of the market range, we reduce the number of buyers just looking at your home, meaning that there's less of a chance of getting an offer and a higher chance of not getting one for an extended period. That could result, if we do get an offer, in it likely being somewhere at the lower end of the price range.

That means you'd have the potential for ending up with less and taking longer to sell than if we price it properly right out of the gate.

So, doesn't it make more sense to price it properly, get it sold in a better time frame and for more money by listing it within the range we've discussed?"

## WILL YOU REDUCE YOUR COMMISSION?

Reply #1

"You obviously need to feel comfortable that the fee being charged is justified by the services being provided, am I right? Let me begin by asking you, how do you feel about everything I've presented to you? (We like it)

May I ask if you're looking for the best bottom line or the lowest commission rate?

As a real estate sales professional, I'm confident that my abilities as a marketer and negotiator will ensure you achieve the highest possible sales price, in the least amount of time adding potentially thousands of dollars to your bottom line. May I show you exactly how working with me will actually net you more? (Demonstrate value and an increase in bottom line) Sound fair?"

Reply #2

"One of the most important reasons to hire a REALTOR® is to negotiate on your behalf to achieve the highest possible price for your property, right?"

If I can't negotiate my own salary, wouldn't you be concerned that I may not be the best negotiator for the sale of your home?"

Reply #3

"I don't charge a commission. Just like your lawyer or dentist, I provide a service and charge a fee for it. I can cut my fees, but I need to know which of the services I provide, which are specifically designed to get your home sold for the most money in the best possible time, would you prefer I not use?"

Reply #4

"Mr. / Mrs. Seller, Let me ask you this. If your boss asked you to do your normal work, but came to you one day and wanted you to do it for a lower salary, how would you feel? Would that be fair? Would you agree?"

## WILL YOU REDUCE YOUR COMMISSION IF MY HOME SELLS QUICKLY?

"Mr. and Mrs. Seller, let me ask you this. Would you pay someone more for doing a good job or a poor job?"

This is a performance based business, which means that the better we perform and the more background work we've done, the shorter time it takes to sell your home.

So what you're saying is that if I do a poor job and take a longer time to sell your home you're willing to pay me more than if I do a good job and sell it faster. Does that make sense to you?"

# FOUNDATIONS FOR SUCCESS
## SYSTEMS CHECKLISTS

## LISTING MANAGEMENT CHECKLIST

MLS #:
Initial Price:
Contract Date:
Expires:
Lockbox:
Added to Market Watch:

**Prior to Appointment**

☐ Pre-Listing Package Delivered 24 - 48 Hrs before appointment
☐ Appointment Confirmed - all decision makers to be present
☐ Seller's Advertising Questionnaire Completed by Seller for Appointment
☐ CMA Completed
☐ Listing Presentation Completed
☐ Current Competitors previewed

**Paperwork to Complete**

☐ Working with a Realtor
☐ Listing Agreement
☐ MLS Data Information Sheet
☐ SPIS
☐ Service Guarantee
☐ FINTRAC Individual Identification Information Record (One per Seller)
☐ Sellers Directions for Offer Presentations & Appointment Info
☐ Seller's Consent & Acknowledgement Form
☐ Taxes Confirmed
☐ Mortgage Verification Form signed

# APPENDIX

- ☐ Mortgage Verification Form sent to bank
- ☐ Mortgage Verification Form returned
- ☐ Survey, if available
- ☐ GeoWarehouse (Ontario) / Title Printout
- ☐ Property History

## Discuss with Seller

- ☐ Seller's Advertising Questionnaire
- ☐ Ideal Closing Date
- ☐ If Winter, do they have summer yard photos?
- ☐ Bridge Financing Discussion
- ☐ Plan for Existing Mortgage
- ☐ Showing Instructions / Times
- ☐ How Office handles Appointments
- ☐ Buyer Showings - What To Do/Not To do
- ☐ Set Agent Open House Date
- ☐ Set First Public Open House Date
- ☐ Offer Management (Date - if holding offers, Handling Bully Offers)
- ☐ Realtor.ca Delay
- ☐ Lawyer Info
- ☐ If Feature Sheets are running low
- ☐ Feedback from Realtors
- ☐ Share Listing with Friends

## Listing Procedures

## Day of Listing Appointment

- ☐ All Paperwork Signed and dated for 2-3 days later
- ☐ Key from the Seller and copy made
- ☐ Book Photographer / Videographer
- ☐ Order Sign
- ☐ Lockbox Installed w/ key

# FOUNDATIONS FOR SUCCESS

- [ ] Files Uploaded to Evernote
- [ ] Files Sent to Office Administrator
- [ ] Enter Client into CRM
- [ ] Enter Files into CRM
- [ ] Enter Listing into Evernote

## Day after Listing

- [ ] Send Letter to Referral
- [ ] Write Ad Copy for Feature Sheets
- [ ] Write Ad Copy for MLS
- [ ] Write Ad Copy for other advertising media
- [ ] Prepare Feature Sheets
- [ ] Design and Print Just Listed Flyer for Home Office
- [ ] Design and Print Just Listed Flyer for RE Offices
- [ ] Design & Print Open House Invitation for Neighbourhood
- [ ] Prepare Thank You Letter
- [ ] Deliver Feature Sheets to Home

## Activation Day

- [ ] Upload on MLS
- [ ] Upload Photos
- [ ] Check MLS for Correct Information
- [ ] E-mail Listing to Clients
- [ ] Upload Virtual Tour
- [ ] Video sent out across social media platforms (Facebook Business Page, YouTube, Instagram, Blog)
- [ ] Video embedded on website
- [ ] Doorknock & Distribute Open House Invitations to neighbours
- [ ] Upload Listing to Kijiji
- [ ] Upload Listing to Housingblock.com
- [ ] Upload Listing to Backpage.ca
- [ ] Upload Listing to Craigslist.ca

# APPENDIX

☐ Email Blast to agents in area

## Weekly Activities

☐ Open House scheduled
☐ Warm calls to neighbours for Open House
☐ Preview Listings in area
☐ Open House held ☐ ☐ ☐ ☐ ☐
☐ Weekly Activity Report completed and sent to Seller ☐ ☐ ☐ ☐ ☐

## Price Reductions

☐ Amendment to Listing Contract signed
☐ Amendment Sent to Office
☐ Price Changed on MLS
☐ Update Blog Post
☐ E-mail Clients
☐ Email sent to all agents who have shown property
☐ Upload Amendment to Evernote
☐ Upload Amendment to CRM

## Multiple Offers

☐ Time set for Offer Presentation
☐ Deadline for Offer Registration set
☐ Every agent notified of new offers
☐ Upload Copy of Each Offer to Evernote
☐ Thank All Agents for their offers

## Conditional Procedures

☐ APS & Confirmation of Co-Operation signed by all parties
☐ Copy of APS & Confirmation of Co-Operation Sent to Client
☐ Deposit Cheque delivered by Purchaser
☐ Deposit Cheque & Paperwork to Deals Secretary (APS, Conf. of Coop., Trade Record)
☐ Upload Copy of Files to Evernote (Cheque, Trade Record, APS)

# FOUNDATIONS FOR SUCCESS

- ☐ Inspection date set & Clients notified
- ☐ Mortgage Condition waived
- ☐ Inspection completed
- ☐ Inspection Condition waived
- ☐ Status Certificate ordered
- ☐ Status Certificate delivered to Purchaser's Agent
- ☐ Status Certificate Condition waived
- ☐ Additional conditions waived
- ☐ Copies of waivers sent to Office
- ☐ Copies of waivers sent to client
- ☐ Upload Copies of waivers to Evernote

**Firm Procedures**

- ☐ Update CRM
- ☐ Update Evernote
- ☐ Send Client Survey
- ☐ Update Website
- ☐ Sold Sign up
- ☐ Remove Lockbox
- ☐ Call for Sign Removal
- ☐ Thank You Gift to Seller
- ☐ Update Closing Date on CRM
- ☐ Move File to Pending Closings
- ☐ Update Trade Record Sheet
- ☐ Update Address for Client in CRM
- ☐ Send Survey to Referral Contact
- ☐ Provide referral to movers if required

**Closing Procedures**

**2 weeks prior to closing**

- ☐ Call Seller's Lawyer to confirm receipt of all paperwork
- ☐ Confirm any repairs required completed

# APPENDIX

- ☐ All receipts left for new owners
- ☐ Buyers' visit scheduled

## 1 week prior to closing

- ☐ Call client to confirm visit with lawyer
- ☐ Confirm movers
- ☐ Thank You Letter
- ☐ File Cheque
- ☐ Send Copy of Feedback to Referral
- ☐ Update CRM
- ☐ Buyers' visit held

## Closing Day

- ☐ Confirm closing with lawyer
- ☐ Move File to Closed Clients Notebook

# FOUNDATIONS FOR SUCCESS
## <u>OPEN HOUSE CHECKLIST</u>

### Monday / Tuesday

- ☐ Open House Scheduled
- ☐ Call the neighbours and invite them to the VIP Open House

### Wednesday

- ☐ Prepare your Open House Gift Bags
- ☐ Inspector Brochure
- ☐ Lawyer Brochure
- ☐ Contractor Brochure
- ☐ Area Information (schools, maps, trails, etc.)
- ☐ Cookie / Bar
- ☐ Prepare Feature Sheets, including Walkscore
- ☐ Prepare Open House Invitations for neighbours

### Thursday

- ☐ Doorknock and distribute Invitations
- ☐ Preview all available listings in area
- ☐ Familiarize yourself with area (schools, transit, shopping, etc.)
- ☐ Organize files needed
- ☐ Feature Sheets
- ☐ Info from Mortgage Broker
- ☐ BRA / Customer Status
- ☐ Sign In Sheets
- ☐ APS
- ☐ Print Labels for Water Bottles

### Friday

- ☐ Buy food and water bottles for VIP Open House

# APPENDIX

## Day of Open House

- ☐ Place signs at intersections and leading to home
- ☐ Sign / flag in front of house
- ☐ Set up food and water
- ☐ Set up laptop with map search
- ☐ Gift Bags out
- ☐ Windows open
- ☐ Doors unlocked
- ☐ Lights On

## After Open House

- ☐ Pick up all flyers, sheets, food
- ☐ Windows closed and locked
- ☐ Doors closed and locked
- ☐ Final walkthrough
- ☐ Note for client
- ☐ Front door locked
- ☐ Collect all signs

# FOUNDATIONS FOR SUCCESS
## <u>BUYER MANAGEMENT CHECKLIST</u>

Client Name:
Phone:

| Home: | Cell: | Work: |
|---|---|---|

Email:
Lawyer's Name:
Phone:
Fax:
Email:
Mortgage Broker:
Phone:
Fax:
Email:

**Prior to Appointment**

☐ Informed Buyer's Guide Delivered 24 - 48 Hrs before appointment

☐ Appointment Confirmed - all decision makers to be present

☐ Buyer's Presentation Completed

**Paperwork to Complete**

☐ Working with a Realtor

☐ Buyer Representation Agreement

☐ FINTRAC Individual Identification Information Record (One per Buyer)

**Discuss with Buyer**

☐ Pre-Approved?   Price Range:

☐ Buyer Questionnaire / Home Buying Wishlist Completed

☐ Ideal Closing Date

# APPENDIX

- ☐ Bridge Financing Discussion
- ☐ Plan for Existing Mortgage
- ☐ What Times are they available for Showings
- ☐ How Offices handle Appointments
- ☐ 6 Step Buying Process
- ☐ "Rules of the Road"
- ☐ Showing Procedures - What To Do / Not To do
- ☐ Set First Showing Date
- ☐ Open House Procedures
- ☐ Offer Management  - sellers holding offers, Bully Offers, negotiating, multiple offers
- ☐ Managing Conditions
- ☐ Lawyer Info
- ☐ Feedback for REALTORS®

## Weekly Activities

- ☐ Preview Listings in area
- ☐ Open Houses viewed ☐ ☐ ☐ ☐
- ☐ Weekly Activity Report completed and sent to Buyer

## Multiple Offers

- ☐ Client notified of Multiple Offers
- ☐ Client given chance to improve offer
- ☐ Time set for Offer Presentation
- ☐ Offer Registered prior to Deadline for Offer Registration
- ☐ Meet clients at location for Offer Presentation
- ☐ Upload Copy of Offer to Evernote

# FOUNDATIONS FOR SUCCESS

**Property Info**

MLS#:

Address:

Offer Date:

Closing:

Condition Date:

Inspection Date:

**Conditional Procedures**

- ☐ APS & Confirmation of Co-Operation signed by all parties
- ☐ Copy of APS & Confirmation of Co-Operation Sent to Client
- ☐ Deposit Cheque delivered to Listing Office
- ☐ Copy of Deposit Cheque, Receipt & Paperwork to Deals Secretary (APS, Conf. of Coop., Trade Record)
- ☐ Upload Copy of Files to Evernote (Cheque, Trade Record, APS)
- ☐ Inspection date set, Listing agent notified
- ☐ APS sent to Financial Institution / Mortgage Broker
- ☐ Mortgage Condition waived
- ☐ Inspection date confirmed 1 day prior
- ☐ Inspection completed
- ☐ Inspection Condition waived & Sent to Listing Agent / Transmission record filed
- ☐ Status Certificate ordered
- ☐ Status Certificate delivered by Listing Agent
- ☐ Status Certificate delivered to Client / Lawyer

# APPENDIX

- ☐ Status Certificate Condition waived & Sent to Listing Agent / Transmission record filed
- ☐ Additional conditions waived & Sent to Listing Agent / Transmission record filed
- ☐ Copies of waivers sent to Office
- ☐ Copies of waivers sent to client
- ☐ Upload Copies of waivers to Evernote

## Firm Procedures

- ☐ Update CRM
- ☐ Update Evernote
- ☐ Send Client Survey
- ☐ Update Website
- ☐ Sold Sign up
- ☐ Update Closing Date on CRM
- ☐ Move File to Pending Closings
- ☐ Update Trade Record Sheet
- ☐ Update Address for Client in CRM
- ☐ Send Survey to Referral Contact
- ☐ Provide referral to movers if required

## Closing Procedures

### 2 weeks prior to closing

- ☐ Call Lawyer to confirm receipt of all paperwork
- ☐ Confirm any repairs required completed
- ☐ All receipts left for new owners
- ☐ Buyers' visit scheduled

# FOUNDATIONS FOR SUCCESS

## 1 week prior to closing

- ☐ Call client to confirm visit with lawyer
- ☐ Confirm movers
- ☐ Thank You Letter
- ☐ File Cheque
- ☐ Send Copy of Feedback to Referral
- ☐ Update CRM
- ☐ Buyers' visit held

## Closing Day

- ☐ Confirm closing with lawyer
- ☐ Meet client at new home
- ☐ Provide lunch for client on moving day
- ☐ Move File to Closed Clients Notebook
- ☐ Implement 1, 1, 1 System

# APPENDIX

## FOUNDATIONS FOR SUCCESS SERIES

**Volume 1 - "On the Right Foot"**
Business Planning, Organization and Real
Estate Etiquette

**Volume 2 - "Good Hunting"**
Prospecting and Lead Follow Up,

**Volume 3 - "Listings, Listings, Listings"**
Listings and Listing Systems,

**Volume 4 - "Buyers, Buyers, Buyers",**
Buyers and Buyers Systems

**Volume 5 - "I'm Just Sayin"**
Objection Handling, Communication and
Negotiation and Advertising

**Volume 6 – The Workbook**
Specific Business Building Exercises

**Volume 7 – The Complete Series**
All the volumes in one book, including the
Workbook.

Purchase individual volumes or the complete series
through the website at
**www.foundationsforsuccess.ca**

# FOUNDATIONS FOR SUCCESS

Steve began his real estate career in Edmonton, Alberta in 2001. He worked as an Associate Broker with Realty Executives North Star until 2008 when he opened his own brokerage. He moved back to Toronto in 2010, has been the Director of Agent Development for HomeLife/Cimerman Real Estate Ltd., Director of Training and Development for RE/MAX West Realty Inc., and Manager and Coach for The Daryl King Team at Royal LePage Your Community Realty and has designed and overseen the training, development and coaching of the sales personnel at each. He is the author of ''List to Last - The Definitive Guide to Finding, Closing and Managing Residential Listings''.

# FOUNDATIONS FOR SUCCESS